Chester
Weirton
Wheeling
New Martinsville
Morgantown
Martinsburg
Charles Town
Fairmont
Parkersburg
Clarksburg
WEST
Winchester
Glenville
Weston
Elkins
Petersburg
VIRGINIA
Point
Pleasant
MONONGAHELA
Spruce Knob
4862
GEORGE
WASHINGTON
NATIONAL FOREST
Warrenton
SHENANDOAH
Alexandria
Triangle
NATIONAL
FOREST
Harrisonburg
Orange
Fredericksburg
Huntington
Charleston
Summersville
Staunton
NATIONAL
Charlottesville
Tappahannock
Richwood
Waynesboro
PARK
Onancock
Logan
Oak Hill
GEORGE WASHINGTON
NATIONAL FOREST
Ashland
Beckley
Hinton
Clifton
Forge
Buena
Vista
VIRGINIA
Richmond
Mullens
Bluestone
Reservoir
JEFFERSON
NATIONAL
Roanoke
Lynchburg
Appomattox
Farmville
Petersburg
Hopewell
Williamsburg
Cape Charles
Prestonsburg
Pikeville
FOREST
Altavista
Blackstone
Waverly
Hampton
Newport News
Welch
JEFFERSON
Radford
Chase City
Norfolk
Bluefield
South
Boston
Emporia
Suffolk
Portsmouth
Richlands
NATIONAL
Martinsville
Danville
Buggs I.
Lake
Dante
FOREST
Galax
Elizabeth City
Norton
Marion
Mount Rogers
5729
Leaksville
Roxboro
Roanoke Rapids
Big Stone Gap
Bristol
Mount Airy
Reidsville
Oxford
Henderson
Ahoskie
Edenton
Elizabethton
Johnson City
Boone
Winston-Salem
Burlington
Louisburg
Scotland
Neck
Williamston
Phelps
Lake
PISGAH
NATIONAL
FOREST
Lenoir
Greensboro
Durham
Raleigh
Rocky Mount
Greenville
Mattamuskeet
Lake
Mount Mitchell
6684
Hickory
High Point
Lexington
Asheboro
Wilson
Asheville
Statesville
Salisbury
NORTH
CAROLINA
Washington
Concord
UWHARRIE
NATIONAL
FOREST
Goldsboro
Kinston
Hendersonville
Shelby
Gastonia
Albemarle
Sanford
Dunn
New Bern
Morehead City
Charlotte
Southern
Pines
CROATAN
NATIONAL
FOREST
Monroe
Rockingham
Fayetteville
Clinton
Jacksonville
Cape Lookout
Lumberton
Whiteville
Wilmington
Cape Fear
ATLANTIC OCEAN

The Border States

TIME-LIFE Library of America

The Border States

**Kentucky North Carolina
Tennessee Virginia West Virginia**

By Wilma Dykeman and James Stokely
and the Editors of
TIME-LIFE BOOKS

TIME-LIFE BOOKS, New York

The Authors: Wilma Dykeman and James Stokely are a writing team who live in Newport, Tennessee, at the edge of the Great Smokies. Both are natives of the Border States— Miss Dykeman is from North Carolina, Mr. Stokely from Tennessee. Since their marriage in 1940 —they had been brought together by Thomas Wolfe's mother and sister—they have collaborated on numerous books and articles dealing with life in their section of the country. Their by-line has appeared in such publications as *The New York Times Magazine, Harper's* and *The New Republic.* In 1958 their book *Neither Black Nor White* received the Hillman Award, given for the best work of the previous year on race relations, civil liberties or world understanding. Miss Dykeman received the 1955 Thomas Wolfe Memorial Award for *The French Broad,* a volume in the "Rivers of America" series. She has also written two novels, *The Tall Woman* and *The Far Family,* and often lectures for college and civic groups on the problems and potentials of the South. Mr. Stokely's poems have appeared in *New South, The Atlantic* and *The Nation* and have been reprinted in high-school and college anthologies.

The Consulting Editor: Oscar Handlin, Charles Warren Professor of American History at Harvard University and director of the university's Charles Warren Center for Studies in American History, is one of America's foremost social historians. His work on U.S. immigrants, *The Uprooted,* won the Pulitzer Prize in 1952.

Border States Consultant: Dewey Wesley Grantham Jr., Professor of History at Vanderbilt University, is the author of *The Democratic South* and has won the Sydnor Award of the Southern Historical Association.

The Cover: Thoroughbred mares and their foals graze at Kentucky's famous Calumet Farm, a leading horse farm and racing stable.

TIME-LIFE BOOKS

Editor
Maitland A. Edey
Executive Editor
Jerry Korn
Text Director   **Art Director**
Martin Mann   Sheldon Cotler
Chief of Research
Beatrice T. Dobie
Picture Editor
Robert G. Mason
Assistant Text Directors:
Harold C. Field, Ogden Tanner
Assistant Art Director:
Arnold C. Holeywell
Assistant Chief of Research:
Martha Turner

Publisher
Rhett Austell
Associate Publisher: Walter C. Rohrer
General Manager: Joseph C. Hazen Jr.
Planning Director: John P. Sousa III
Circulation Director: Joan D. Manley
Marketing Director: Carter Smith
Business Manager: John D. McSweeney
Publishing Board: Nicholas Benton,
Louis Bronzo, James Wendell Forbes

TIME-LIFE Library of America

Series Editor: Oliver E. Allen
Editorial Staff for *The Border States:*
Assistant Editor: William Frankel
Picture Editor: Susan Rayfield
Designer: John Newcomb
Assistant Designer: Jean Lindsay
Staff Writers: Tony Chiu, Lee Greene,
Marianna Kastner, Frank Kendig,
Victor Waldrop
Chief Researcher: Clara E. Nicolai
Text Research: Ruth Silva, Marian Taylor,
Doris Coffin, Louise Samuels
Picture Research: Nancy Jacobsen,
Rhea Finkelstein, Elizabeth Evans,
Johanna Zacharias, Margo Dryden,
Myra Mangan

Editorial Production
Color Director: Robert L. Young
Assistant: James J. Cox
Copy Staff: Marian Gordon Goldman,
Susan Galloway, Patricia Miller,
Florence Keith
Picture Department: Dolores A. Littles,
Marquita Jones
Traffic: Arthur A. Goldberger
Art Assistants: Jean Held, Dirk Laninga

The text of this book was written by Wilma Dykeman and James Stokely, the picture essays by the editorial staff. Valuable aid was provided by the following individuals and departments of Time Inc.: LIFE staff photographers Alfred Eisenstaedt and John Dominis; Editorial Production, Robert W. Boyd Jr.; Editorial Reference, Peter Draz; Picture Collection, Doris O'Neil; Photographic Laboratory, George Karas; TIME-LIFE News Service, Richard M. Clurman; Correspondents Charles Connor (Charleston, W. Va.), Dwayne Walls (Charlotte, N.C.), James Latimer (Richmond, Va.), Warner Ogden (Knoxville, Tenn.), John Fetterman (Louisville, Ky.), Wayne Whitt (Nashville, Tenn.), Jay Jenkins (Raleigh, N.C.) and Thomas BeVier (Memphis, Tenn.).

Contents

Introduction

This book captures the spirit of one region of America—a spirit of pride, of adventure and of a pioneering intent. It is the spirit of a people pushing constantly onward, from the time when they first sought better lives by moving westward and challenging the mountains; and it is this spirit, more than anything else, that characterizes the region.

A region is always many regions. In the Border States—the states of Virginia, West Virginia, North Carolina, Kentucky and Tennessee—there are at least four different regions: a plantation country along the coast, a hilly plateau country called the Piedmont, the high peaks and mountain country of the Appalachians, and a second plantation country in the Mississippi Valley. It is no easy job to relate a coastal city like Norfolk, Virginia, to a mountain city like Charleston, West Virginia, or to show how either of these communities fits in with the great Mississippi River town of Memphis. Yet they all belong to one region, and what unifies the region is the spirit of the people who live in it. These people are perhaps the purest representation of the original settlers of this country that can be found today. In this book, more than anything else, Wilma Dykeman and James Stokely have celebrated the people of the Border States— their optimism and ambition, their hardiness and their willingness to try new things.

They have also recorded the adversities these people have faced, particularly in the last hundred years or so. I can add my own testimony to their record, for I spent my youth in a small North Carolina town during the years of the Great Depression, and for the most part it was an experience of poverty, of suffering and of lack of opportunity.

Within the Border States, my town was some-thing of a border community, lying between the coastal plantation country on one side and the industrialized Piedmont on the other. By tradition, one section looked back to the glories of the antebellum plantation days; the other looked forward to an industrialized future. Yet both sections were poverty-stricken; both were insecure. And though my people belonged neither to the most affluent nor the most deprived groups in our community, I soon came to recognize my town's poverty and insecurity.

We always had a garden, and every spring and summer I pulled a handcart through what we called New Town (which was where the black people lived, and it was anything but new) to sell collard greens and peas, tomatoes and okra. I remember the muddy roads I had to cross to get there, and the ramshackle houses, the outdoor toilets, the filth and litter in the yards, the stripped-down, useless automobiles scattered about. The people of New Town lived in a condition of hopelessness, with almost no chance of decent jobs or a satisfying life. You could hire a maid for 75 cents a week, and the family that paid three or four dollars a week had by far the most prestigious situation in the town (as did the maid, or cook, as we called them in those times). The men had pickup jobs of one kind or another, usually for a few dollars a week, at the most.

On the other side of where I lived, beginning about a half block away, was a company-owned mill town. There, too, I saw poverty and hopelessness. The houses were little better than those of New Town; there was no running water, but only a single hand pump in the middle of each block, and no electricity, but only kerosene lamps. And I remember the whistle that blew every morning and evening at 6 o'clock, calling the millworkers to their 12-hour shifts and sending them home again. I remember the mill boys and girls who came to school. Almost always, after the first or second grades, they would be a grade or two behind, and sitting in what then was called the "slow section." They hardly ever brought lunches, and at that time you either brought your own lunch or had no lunch. And ultimately they sort of disappeared from school, and we would recognize them afterward as being dropouts somewhere along the way. Here again were people living without hope for their future or the future of their children.

Finally, there was the farming community. Most farmers lived on the ragged edge of disaster. By necessity, the majority were sharecroppers, dependent on a landowner (who was not really very well off, either) for land and mules and fertilizer and food. Even the few farmers who owned their own land lived in constant fear of the one bad year that could wipe them out.

As I look back, then, I see the three major segments of my boyhood community living in poverty and raising their children in environments that simply could not foster ambition or achievement. What is more, the weaknesses of my part of North Carolina were only part of the weakness of the whole state, just as weakness in any part of the nation reflects weakness in the nation as a whole.

In some respects, perhaps, we had betrayed the dreams upon which the Border States were founded. We had crossed the mountains and settled the land, but we had failed to cross a mountain of neglect—neglect of natural resources and human capacity. The lack of individual opportunity had led to a lack of regional achievement, and our five states were near the bottom in the range of national income and educational stan-

dards. In some way, we had let America slip past us.

For my generation, the agonizing dilemmas of the Border States presented the greatest challenge we could ever face. To catch up with the rest of the nation, we had to innovate; while other regions were steadily progressing, we had to take great leaps. Essentially, our problem was one of human development, and in my own view our enduring need was wider and more effective education. Good education is not simply a matter of hiring more teachers or paying higher salaries or doing more of what has already been done. We must give young people an education that will not only create self-respect but also produce citizens who contribute to their community and the nation. Above all, we need an imaginative approach to education—to an education that reaches every child, that seeks out every talent, that fundamentally alters the traditional view of the educative process.

As this incisive and far-ranging book makes clear, such innovations are possible in the Border States. The region's people have inherited a proud tradition—the tradition of the pioneer spirit that pushed across the mountains and opened up the West. With this pride and this pioneering tradition we can catch up with the rest of America by releasing the potential of our human resources. We can help our people to grow and to seek or make their opportunities. The Border States, largely populated with the descendants of the men and women—red and white and black—who originally settled America, have the native ability that is needed to upgrade this oldest of our nation's regions. The challenge is there, the capacity is there, and the future of the region is bright.

—TERRY SANFORD
Former Governor of North Carolina

1

A Spacious, Secret Land

From its beginning the land of the Border States has been a paradox. It has been rich and fruitful, yet austere and demanding; as bright and beckoning as the glint of sun on white sand and salt water, yet as dark and forbidding as the layers of shadows deepening scooped-out valleys between rugged mountains.

As the land is paradoxical, so, too, are the people who live on it. From the start they built with both proud brick and humble log—and relics of each survive, in the elegance of colonial Tryon Palace on the North Carolina coast and in the simplicity of Harrodsburg fort on the site of the first permanent white settlement in Kentucky. At Charlottesville, Virginia, they established the most "aristocratic" state university in the nation, where young men could learn to fit the mold of the Virginia gentleman; yet at Berea, Kentucky, they created one of the most "democratic" private colleges in the country, where every student needs financial help and none pays tuition, and where everyone does manual as well as academic work.

In a mountain cove of eastern Kentucky, a farmer plows his patch of bottomland. Flat land is rare in this part of the Border States; to feed their families, many mountain farmers cultivate steep slopes like the one in the background.

The people of the Border States are not half-measure people. They like their horses fast, their drinks hard and their preaching hell-fire hot. They have proved themselves the most quixotic visionaries—and the most pragmatic of realists. One border state, West Virginia, was the setting for the activities of two figures whose roles in American history covered the range from utter extremism to utter accommodation. The first was John Brown, the fanatic of Harpers Ferry fame, whose equally fanatical contemporary, the Reverend Henry Ward Beecher, wrote: "Let no man pray that Brown be spared. Let Virginia make him a martyr. Now he has only blundered. His cause was noble; his work miserable. But a cord and a gibbet would redeem all that, and round up Brown's failure with a heroic success." The other figure was Booker T. Washington, born a slave in Virginia, whose freedom-loving stepfather escaped to West Virginia. Between his emancipation and his death in 1915, Booker T. Washington became the spokesman for American Negroes by virtue of his ability to muster both white and Negro support in the context of his times, using compromise to win dangerous and important struggles.

This Border States' combination of enthusiasm and realism was best reflected, perhaps, in the reminiscence of one resident: "My grandfather was a mighty man in theology in his day. He knocked out his opponents and he battered the devil. My father was a lawyer and a soldier. He fought the United States by argument and in war. I notice that the devil and the United States are both doing business yet. I made up my mind, therefore, that I would change the family job and do what I can to build mills and roads."

Such a wry view of existence comes naturally in a region that cherishes the art of the raconteur, the teller of tales and anecdotes. On summer lawns and wide verandas, at crossroads stores and country courthouses, at religious revival meetings and family reunions, there have invariably been storytellers who could make life a little larger and more enjoyable, temper opposition with laughter and reduce a potential fight to a joke. And along with this gregarious humorist, the people of the Border States have also honored the resourceful individualist—the man who could take the hardships of ruinous seasons on the farms or setbacks in business and career and still laugh.

Nowhere in the United States has there been more continuous homage given to the niceties of courtesy and polite society than in portions of the Border States—yet this conformity of manners has been matched by an equally vigorous nonconformity. Elaborate chivalry and urbane sophistication have co-existed with the more awkward etiquette of the Davy Crocketts. Adam O'Brien, a wandering pioneer during the early settlement of western Virginia, may have been the prototype for all the rugged nonconformists. When O'Brien in the early 1800s felt himself crowded out of breathing space by new settlers and growing towns, he attacked "those varmints, the sheriffs and constables" who were "worse than Indians, because you can kill Indians and you dare not kill the sheriffs." Those who had come earlier, he said, had "lived quite happy before the Revolution, for then there was no law, no courts and no sheriffs and they agreed pretty well, but after awhile the people began to come and made settlements and then there was need for laws; and then came the lawyers and next the preachers, and from that time they never had any peace anymore."

"Natural feeling"—a readiness to love or hate, to support or oppose, to praise or condemn—has been characteristic of the Border States people. Personal or local relationships are still more important than public relations. To look at any single example of this "natural feeling" is to recog-

nize both an asset and a debit. State pride, for example, probably continues to linger at its most brilliant—or its most virulent—in Virginia. (Author William Cabell Bruce made a tart commentary on his fellow Virginians when he said, "No one should ever ask a man whether he was born in Virginia because, if he was, he certainly will tell you himself, and if he was not, he will be ashamed to admit it.") Pride of state can be admirable and may lead to progress—or to a dangerous astigmatism. The latter was illustrated by the response of a governor of Virginia to a question about the gullied roads and eroded hillsides of his state. He vowed that he would no more quarrel with these furrows on the land than "with the wrinkles on [his] old mother's brow."

Yet for all its flaws, the pride of the Border States people has managed to embrace most of the paradoxes of their characters. At bottom, it is a pride in and an understanding of the land, for most of the region's paradoxes have arisen from three facts about its geography—facts which have shaped its past and its present styles of life.

First, the Border States region is a land bounded by big waters—the Atlantic Ocean to the east, the Potomac and Ohio Rivers to the north and northwest, the Mississippi to the west—ebbing, flowing, carrying the world's commerce in and out. But it is also a land dominated by a mighty system of mountains—the lofty Appalachians, long folded in isolation, upthrust like a giant backbone running down the middle of the region. The sea and the rivers have given rise to rootlessness, restless dreams and yearnings and nostalgias, the music of "Shenandoah" and the riverman's cry, "Mark twain!" The hills have bred other longings and voices, and the music of "Cumberland Gap," "Old Smoky" and "Lonesome Valley."

Second, part of this region was historically a border between East and West—between an America still bound to Europe by ties of ancestry and culture, and a raw wilderness country discovering its own identity. This East-West distinction was most important during colonial times and the early years of the nation, when the interior of the Border States was still called the Old Southwest.

Third, the region has always been a border area between the Deep South and the North. The conflicts between its neighboring regions, which erupted in open warfare during the Civil War, are far from resolved today. They are still reflected in Border States politics. When V. O. Key wrote his definitive study, *Southern Politics*, he discov-

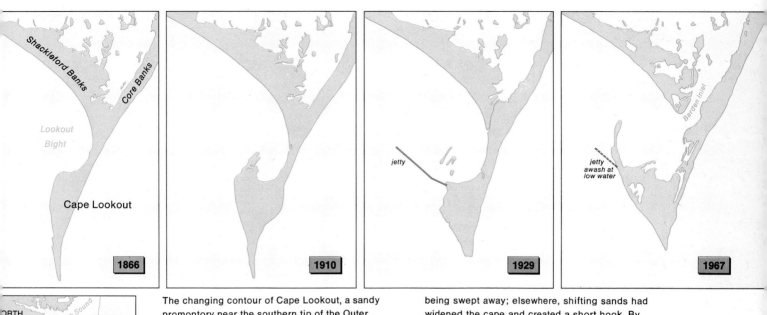

maps labeled 1866, 1910, 1929, 1967 and inset map of North Carolina

Shackleford Banks

Core Banks

Lookout Bight

Cape Lookout

1866

1910

jetty

1929

Barden Inlet

jetty awash at low water

1967

ORTH ROLINA — Pamlico Sound — Cape Hatteras — *Atlantic Ocean* — slow Bay — Cape Lookout

The changing contour of Cape Lookout, a sandy promontory near the southern tip of the Outer Banks of North Carolina, reflects the forces of wind and wave that created and constantly reshape these offshore reefs. In a chart made in 1866 the cape appears as a strip of sand protecting a bay called Lookout Bight. By 1910 the cape's tip was being swept away; elsewhere, shifting sands had widened the cape and created a short hook. By 1929 the hook had disappeared, possibly washed away by a storm, and a jetty had been built to make a safe harbor in the bight. Most of this jetty was buried by 1967, and water had broken through the north shore of the bight, forming Barden Inlet.

ered that in an otherwise predominantly Democratic region, the Appalachian Mountains formed a "great spine of Republicanism which runs down the back of the South." Sevier County, Tennessee, bordering the Great Smokies, was a strong area of Unionist sentiment during the Civil War, in spite of the fact that it was in a Confederate state. Today it still votes one of the heaviest Republican majorities of any county in the nation.

The geographical contrasts in the Border States —the ever-present tensions between water and mountains, East and West, North and South— have so shaped the region's character that they provide the clues to an understanding of it. The first of these three geographical tensions will be discussed in this chapter (the second and third will be taken up in later chapters), for this basic tension between waters and mountains established the earliest, and in many ways the sharpest, division in the five states.

"There's water and earth, and during Creation the Lord divided them one from the other," a North Carolina mountain woman said after a trip to the opposite end of the state to "view" the ocean. "I'm of the notion that we're divided up that way, too: into water folks and hill folks. There's some that are smothered by mountains.

And there's others that the sea unsettles. I'm at home on the land—leveled out or piled up, it's no hardship to me—but I'm a true stranger to water and water's ways."

Not only in this hill woman's mind are land and water in conflict. Their relentless struggle has been recorded through the geologic ages. The ceaseless bite and flow of water chiseled the profile of the land and the contours of the mountains, and by the massive resistance of the land the watercourses of rivers were charted.

When Europeans first saw this land the division between water and mountain had existed for millions of years. But the first settlers tried to ignore it. In the beginning, the region was all Virginia. By its royal charter of 1609, Virginia reached from the Atlantic to the Pacific and from a latitude deep in present South Carolina to a point within the present boundaries of Pennsylvania. Since then Virginia has shrunk considerably, but it is still called "the mother of states," and the roll call of the states it has mothered includes all five of today's Border States. Two of these, North Carolina, touching sea and mountains, and Tennessee, linking the mountains to the Mississippi, are long parallelograms, with North Carolina narrowing irregularly at its western end where it joins Tennessee. Sea-oriented Virginia and the hilly plateau of Kentucky are irregular triangles, each sloping to a rough point at its western boundary. And mountain-locked West Virginia sprawls like a spread-eagled frog, with one narrow leg pushing north between Ohio and Pennsylvania, the other leg stretched east between Maryland and Virginia, and the bulk of its plump body swelling south between Kentucky and Virginia.

But it is as a region, rather than as a group of political entities, that the Border States most clearly reveal their water-mountain contrast. Traversing them from east to west, one goes from water to mountains to water again.

The Border States begin at the Atlantic shore, where a part of the great coastal plain of eastern North America stretches from the broad expanse of Virginia's Chesapeake Bay down to the narrow treacherous islands of North Carolina's Outer Banks. This seaboard, known to Virginians as the "Tidewater" and to North Carolinians merely as the "Coast," includes both a terrain and a history that are unique in the nation. Here English-speaking America was born. Here the founding fathers fought and argued and in immense travail and patience outlined a pattern for a nation's destiny.

Four major rivers—the Potomac, the Rappahannock, the York and the James—enter Chesapeake Bay in broad estuaries, cutting Virginia's coastal plain into three strips, or "necks." Along these necks arose the American colonies' first plantations, where family dynasties took root and flourished. The story of these plantations is intertwined with that of the nation itself. Historian Clifford Dowdey has described one of them, Berkeley Hundred on the James River, with a characteristically Virginian sprinkling of genealogy: "Berkeley Hundred, a working plantation still in operation after three and one-half centuries, is older than any English-speaking settlement in America outside Virginia. In fact, a Thanksgiving was celebrated on its river front and an experiment made there with corn whiskey before the Puritans, setting sail in one of the boats bound for Virginia, were blown off their course and landed in New England. . . . Berkeley evolved out of the wilderness to become the demesne of the Harrisons [who included] presidents of the United States, governors of Virginia, a Signer of the Declaration of Independence and an ancestor of Robert E. Lee. The Harrisons helped shape their immediate region into one of the most powerful and fabled sections of Virginia. Their home

place sat between the Westover of William Byrd and the Shirley of the Hills and Carters; President John Tyler lived nearby, and his brief term as William Henry Harrison's vice-president was probably the only time in the country's history when a president and his vice-president had grown up in the same neighborhood. The wife of George Washington and of Thomas Jefferson came from that section, and Lee's mother was born there."

In addition to its three necks, the Tidewater also includes the Eastern Shore, a narrow 62-mile peninsula between the bay and the ocean. Made accessible in recent years by the 17.6-mile-long Chesapeake Bay Bridge-Tunnel, the Eastern Shore is deeply rural. Migrant labor camps dot fertile farmlands that produce a variety of vegetables, especially potatoes.

At the northern end of the Tidewater lie Alexandria, Arlington and their adjoining suburbs, all bedroom communities for Washington, D.C. The area is characterized by traffic cloverleafs, burgeoning apartment houses, mushrooming subdivisions—and the Pentagon. And at the southern end of the Tidewater, near the Virginia-North Carolina line, is the commodious harbor of Hampton Roads, comprising 50 miles of shoreline that serves Norfolk (Virginia's largest city), Portsmouth and Newport News. Concentrated in this busy area (the natural harbor is perhaps the finest between New York and Rio de Janeiro) is one of the world's greatest shipbuilding, maritime, military and aviation complexes.

In North Carolina the coast changes dramatically. Beautiful, dangerous, deceptive, this 320-mile seafront, known to seafarers as the "graveyard of the Atlantic," provides an example of geography's influence on history. As one historian has pointed out, "The treacherous coast and lack of good ports were major factors in diverting English colonization to the Chesapeake region. . . . The colony was settled largely 'as an overflow from other colonies,' notably Virginia, South Carolina, and Pennsylvania. These same geographic factors operated throughout the nineteenth century to the detriment of North Carolina's economic development, and even in the twentieth century the state is still trying to overcome these natural obstacles."

The North Carolina coast begins in a chain of long, narrow barrier reefs, curved like an elbow thrust out into the ocean. These are the Outer Banks, lonely stretches of sea and sand broken by occasional small fishing villages. According to folklore, the "Bankers" are descendants of pirates who once found harbor here and of early colonists shipwrecked here. Historical records prove the presence of pirates: on Ocracoke Island, Edward Teach, better known as Blackbeard, was killed during a bloody encounter in 1718. And both history and the remains of hapless vessels still bleaching on the dunes confirm the tales of shipwreck. A narrow spit of sand called Nags Head allegedly received its name from land-pirates who, on stormy nights, hung a lantern around a nag's neck and with the moving light lured ships to the treacherous shore—and their death.

The Outer Banks are a land where savage hurricanes strike and tropical plants thrive; where wild ponies race in the salty breeze and tame tourists brown in the sun; where sturdy yaupon and delicate sea oats grow. Here, in 1953, the first National Seashore was established at Cape Hatteras, and here, too, the air age was born. At Kill Devil Hills, on a windy morning in December 1903, Orville Wright piloted the first mechanically driven, heavier-than-air machine over a distance of some 100 feet above a stretch of level sand.

In addition to its Outer Banks, North Carolina's coast has three distinct capes jutting out into the ocean. These capes, called Hatteras, Lookout and Fear, mark the sea lane entrances to the state's chief port towns, Morehead City, Beaufort and Wilmington. It was Cape Fear, at the mouth of the meandering river of that name, that inspired a famous description by George Davis, the Attorney General of the Confederacy: "The kingdom of silence and awe, disturbed by no sound save the seagull's shriek and the breakers' roar.... Imagination cannot adorn it. Romance cannot hallow it. Local pride cannot soften it. There it stands today, bleak and threatening and pitiless.... And as its nature, so its name, is now, always has been and always will be the Cape of Fear."

Between the Outer Banks and the mainland are five sounds, of which the largest are Albemarle and Pamlico. Into the sounds, too shallow for commercial shipping, empty most of the rivers draining North Carolina's wide coastal plain. Where the rivers broaden and merge with the waters of the sounds, deep swamplands cover the coasts. They are called by the natives "dismals," and the major example is the extensive area known as the Great Dismal Swamp, which extends from North Carolina into southern Virginia. There are also numerous lakes in the area; the

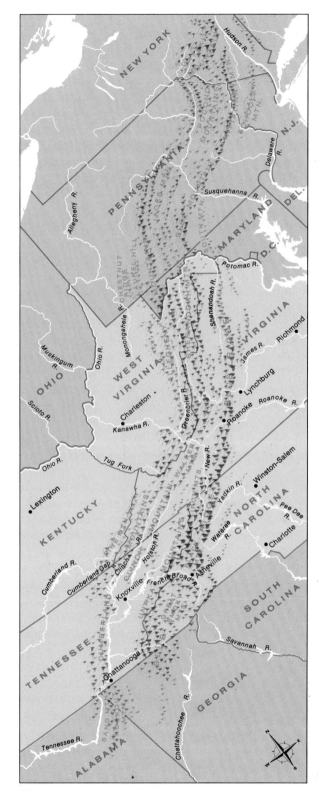

The mountain ranges making up the vast Appalachian chain have their highest peaks within the Border States. For many years these barriers played a decisive role in the history of the region by keeping colonists in the eastern lowlands. The discovery of such passes as the Cumberland Gap enabled settlers to make their way west into Kentucky and Tennessee.

largest, Mattamuskeet, covers some 65 square miles. As far back as colonial times, this country of fresh and salt waters, grass-covered savannas, marshes and swamps has lured hunters and fishermen.

Part of the original wealth of the coastal plain was in its pine trees. These magnificent forests furnished naval stores for England's needs; the export of tar, pitch, rosin and turpentine became a major industry in North Carolina and Virginia, and North Carolina's tar gave rise to its nickname, the Tar Heel State. After the pines were cut down, the land was easily cultivated, and with little water power and few mineral resources, the area came to depend on agriculture. Plantations grew up, and slavery shaped a way of life here as it never did in the other areas of the state.

Between the coastal plain of the east and the Appalachians to the west lies the Piedmont ("foot of the mountains") Plateau of Virginia and North Carolina, spreading like a fan from a width of 40 miles at the Potomac to its widest spread of 200 miles in central North Carolina. At the eastern rise of the Piedmont is the fall line, where the streams that rise on the mountain slopes pass from the hard rocks of the west to the softer formations of the coastal plain, carving out picturesque waterfalls and rapids. These fast-moving waters provide the power for the constantly expanding industry of the Piedmont. In this area, too, there is Virginia's Albemarle County, one of the wealthiest counties in America. Once famous as the home of the Albemarle Pippin, Queen Victoria's favorite apple, it is now the heart of a fashionable hunt country. Pink coats, which are really red; hunt breakfasts, which are actually half-luncheons; and an understated affluence that certifies large reservoirs of wealth—all these characterize the strenuous leisure of Albemarle's country estates, where riding is a way of life.

North Carolina's Piedmont has more people and more money than any other part of the state. Charlotte, Greensboro and Winston-Salem, the only cities in the state with more than 100,000 people, are all in the Piedmont. North Carolina's three major industries—tobacco, textiles and furniture—are all centered in the Piedmont. The state's largest and most famous educational institutions are here, too. And in a small strip of the southern Piedmont called the Sandhills are the golf and riding meccas of Pinehurst and Southern Pines.

The Piedmont is intermediate, different from the coast, yet not of the mountains. But farther west the country—and life—change abruptly. In perpetual contrast to the low, salt-water, steamy summertime spread of the coastal plain in the east, there rise the green spring-fed slopes and cloud-wrapped heights of the mountains at the heart of the Border States region.

"It's a great life for dogs and men but it's hard on women and steers"—thus one writer summarized the hardships of mountain life. The mountains confront men with an exhausting terrain and a proving ground for fortitude; they also offer unexpected pleasures and unparalleled beauties. The Appalachians slant south and west along the border of Virginia and West Virginia, through eastern Kentucky and across eastern Tennessee and western North Carolina. In an immense and violent drama, enacted over a period of some 500 million years, towering mountains formed and nameless seas buckled and disappeared. Intense heat and powerful pressures thrust the earth up and folded it together again. Then water became the instrument by which these ranges were carved: rivulets and streams and inland seas shaped rock so old that it reveals no trace of life. Slowly, however, invertebrates and fishes, plants and animals, ferns and the first amphibians, brought life to the bleak landscape.

In "Old Appalachia," with the Blue Ridge at its heart, the mountains have stood much as they are today for some 200 million years. "New Appalachia" includes the younger ranges, notably the Alleghenies and the Cumberlands, lying west of the Great Appalachian Valley (called the Shenandoah Valley in Virginia and the Tennessee Valley to the southwest). Here many of the rich coal beds of the world were laid down during the Carboniferous period of fern and conifer forest and the great reptiles. These seams of coal now shape the human life of the region. In addition to coal, quantities of other organic fuels, oil and natural gas, were created. And deposits of salt provided the base for West Virginia's great Kanawha Valley chemical industry.

The Appalachians were old when the Sierras and the Rockies were born, and the waters of the ages have worn them down to gentler contours than those of the younger Western ranges. When glaciers from the great Ice Ages pushed south, they never reached the southern Appalachians. Plant life clung to these Appalachians as a last refuge and was preserved there to reseed the northern parts of the continent after the ice slowly retreated.

Equally important, a thick soil cover, formed by the long decay of rock, remained on the highland (elsewhere, melting glaciers washed the cover off), so that a deep residual soil blanketed much of the Southern mountains. Today the region's forests support a remarkable plant life, characteristic of both the North and South.

On the boundary of North Carolina and Tennessee runs the dividing line of the segment of the Appalachians included in the Great Smoky Mountains National Park, the most popular national park in the country. A unique feature of the park's history is the fact that it was not set aside by the federal government from lands already in the public domain, as were most of the national parks. It was a gift, not from the government to the people, but from the people to the government. Donations ranging from school children's coins to five million dollars from the Laura Spelman Rockefeller Memorial, and appropriations by Tennessee, North Carolina and the federal government, all contributed to the final purchase of the land for this national park, some 800 square miles of the wildest highlands in eastern America.

The influence of the Appalachians on history and daily life is nowhere more apparent than in West Virginia. This state, sometimes called "the Switzerland of America," is almost entirely mountainous. Its agriculture has always been limited, and communications have posed a major problem. From its hill-bound university in Morgantown to its luxurious resort at White Sulphur Springs, West Virginia is a land of hills and valleys, a land once completely covered with forest. The state also contains some of those bogs identified as Southern muskegs, where fascinating remnants of plant and animal life from the Ice Age still flourish. Here, too, are the steep shaly ridges called shale barrens, home of rare ferns and orchids, white birch and beach-heath, and the rapidly disappearing golden eagle.

The mountains are also pre-eminent in the eastern quarter of Kentucky, a sloping plateau where the Cumberland and Pine Mountain ranges form steep valleys and sharp ridges. It is an area of small valley farms and tilted acres of subsistence grubbing, of scenic canyons and natural rock arches, of laurel and azalea and tulip trees. Above all—or underlying all—it is coal country, a store of natural wealth so exploited that the region is a dark rural pocket of the nation's poverty. Its people make it a reservoir of individualism and contentiousness, of friendliness and fundamentalism,

of old rhythms colliding with the brisk functionalism of a mass-produced world.

Beyond the mountains, stretching westward, Kentucky and Tennessee slant down through the famous rolling Bluegrass country to the rich river plains of the Ohio and Mississippi. There is a folk saying that when an east Kentuckian dies he wants to go to Lexington, the heart of that most hallowed of the state's kingdoms, the Bluegrass. The city boasts the state university and more than 200 horse farms in the surrounding countryside. Kentucky's other major city, Louisville, and its capital Frankfort, are also in the Bluegrass country. This is an area of gregarious people, whose sociability culminates annually during the week of Louisville's Kentucky Derby, in May. There are those who think that the horses' run for the blanket of roses may be the least strenuous aspect of Derby Week, with its daily and nightly round of festivities, and its never ending succession of Kentucky ham, beaten biscuits and mint juleps.

Between the Bluegrass and the Ohio River stretches a subregion peculiar to Kentucky: the Pennyrile. (Its name derives from the pennyroyal, a mint plant common in the area.) In the Pennyrile are giant Mammoth Cave (and countless other underground caverns), Fort Knox with its multibillion dollar horde of federal gold reserves, and —where the Green River flows into the Ohio—one of the world's finest migratory bird routes.

Between the mountains and the Mississippi, Tennessee, too, has rolling midlands that stretch southward from Kentucky with much the same basic formations and textures. In fact, although Kentucky is called the Bluegrass State, Tennessee has about as many acres of bluegrass as Kentucky, providing a nourishing cover and year-round grazing. In both states, bluegrass has helped to produce esteemed strains of horses; Kentucky is famous for its Thoroughbred race horses, Tennessee for Tennessee Walking Horses, which are raised on stock farms in the vicinity of Shelbyville.

Nashville is an industrial city, a financial and educational center, the state's political capital and the world's country music capital. As the "Athens of the South" it boasts a replica of the Parthenon, Vanderbilt and Fisk Universities, George Peabody College for Teachers, and the Cheekwood Art Museum. It looks with condescension on east Tennessee (especially Knoxville) as uncouth, and on west Tennessee (especially Memphis) as upstart.

At the city of Memphis, on the bluffs overlooking the Mississippi River, the Border States reach their westernmost point. Here the Old South and the Old Southwest meet. Memphis is the trading center of Tennessee's cotton kingdom, which has had more in common with neighboring Mississippi and Arkansas than with the distant upland sections of its own state. There is a saying that the Mississippi delta country begins in the lobby of Memphis' Peabody Hotel and ends at Vicksburg.

Born as a river boom town, Memphis has grown to become the largest city in the Border States. It is a major cotton market, despite diversification to other crops and to livestock, and a major hardwood shipping center. But its deepest significance, perhaps, still stems from its symbolic position at the farthest western border of the Border States. The city's Top of the 100 Club, at the summit of a skyscraper, has a circular, glass-enclosed cocktail lounge that revolves slowly. During the course of a leisurely conversation, a visitor may take a long slow look at the 360-degree view surrounding Memphis. New buildings punctuate the level landscape: a sombrero-shaped stadium, a coliseum, a federal building and the city hall. In the evening, as the glass walls complete their orbit, a red sun disappears over the half-mile-wide Mississippi. Beyond the river the west stretches away, flat and beckoning. The distance from the Atlantic Coast, with its thundering waves, past the pine-scented Piedmont, over the green heights of the Appalachians and across the fertile Bluegrass to the broad Mississippi seems all of its 800-odd miles. From sea to river, the region holds yesterday in revered corners and pushes out toward tomorrow in expanding cities, and the space and tensions between water and mountains, between East and West, and between North and South, seem enormous.

Yet despite these tensions, there are strong ties unifying the region. One Virginian has described the paradox of a diversity that ends in a sense of unity: "The regional culture of Tidewater, the Piedmont and the mountain country varies widely, even to accents; and interests of the three sections not infrequently clash head on. But...the variety of the regions forms for the Virginian a physical self-sufficiency within his own borders which goes a long way toward explaining his character."

Numerous factors enter into this sense of self-sufficiency and unity. There is a dominant Anglo-Saxon ancestry; there is a strong feeling for the land, even among urban dwellers; and there is the collective memory of a brutal war fought largely within the region. But perhaps the most potent unifying force throughout the region remains an allegiance to family. This allegiance is as strong in the mountains as in the Tidewater, and it has continued to survive—a trifle daunted, perhaps, but by no means vanquished—despite all the disruptive influences that shatter family ties everywhere.

Historian Clifford Dowdey has ascribed this sense of family to the majority of his fellow Virginians: "The center of Virginia's parochial society has always been the family—indeed, the state is something of a family. The basis of this is not, as is commonly thought, 'ancestor worship,' though certainly there are awesome bores on the subject. . . . The family is simply the thing of value, as is wealth . . . in a money society."

An authority on Kentuckiana has pointed out that to the native of the state, history centers on his family. "When his ancestors crossed the Appalachians, the family was the core of community life and the Kentuckian has never lost sight of the importance of his family attachment."

And during a conversation in his Charleston office, a West Virginian told some recent visitors: "Consider the fact that from late June through each October our newspaper—and I'll lay wagers on this—prints more notices of family reunions than any other paper in the country....One family I know in an adjoining county has thousands who come to their reunion each year. Fifty thousand were reported by the wire services one year! It's like a gathering of the clans."

The people of the Border States have, on occasion, seemed to extend this sense of family to an appropriation of American history. Perhaps their pride is pardonable; they are sensitive to what often seems to them an overemphasis on the New England-Puritan national heritage. They like to point out that America began here, with the intrepid little English-speaking settlement on the James River in 1607; that the region has provided 13 Presidents of the United States; that it was the site of surrender for the two major wars fought on American soil; and that it gave birth to the first, and continuing, popular world image of the American frontiersman, that legendary hero of indestructible proportions.

The region's past has been spirited and touched with honor. Its future is ripe with possibility. And the attitude of many of its people might still be that of a North Carolina editor who always had strong opinions and expressed them vigorously. Once, when he was proved wrong on an issue, he admitted his mistake, and added, "But I would rather be wrong than nothing."

Evening mists soften forested mountaintops in the Great Smokies.

A world of woods and water

Locked in the Appalachian Mountains, which run through the Border States like a giant knobby backbone, is some of the most beautiful country in America. It is a country of high peaks, wild waters and thick forests. Spring-fed rills flow down steep slopes to form turbulent streams; cascades and rapids alternate with still pools where trout glide silently through the shadows. The tangled woods shelter nearly 4,000 varieties of plant life, along with whole menageries of birds, deer and bears.

Today, the wild beauty of this land is seriously threatened. In Kentucky, Tennessee, Virginia and West Virginia, strip miners have ruined some 300,000 acres of mountainside; on Kentucky's magnificent Red River, a proposed dam would destroy nearly 3,500 acres of an irreplaceable gorge. To preserve the kind of wilderness shown in these pictures, conservationists are fighting to put an end to such devastation.

A willow tatters in spring floods.

A stream tumbles down a passage of ledges.

Lichen and maple leaves spatter a tree trunk.

Branches outspread, a maple salutes the spring.

Cool in the shade, a white-tailed deer waters at a still pool.

In a hush of deep woods, a bumblebee attacks a white laurel blossom *(top),* and a trout slips upstream *(bottom).*

A fragile cover of wild blue phlox carpets a forest floor in West Virginia.

A natural bridge, carved from rock by eons of erosion, spans a chasm.

Dwarfed by a rocky ledge, a hiker works his way down the Red River Gorge.

On a high, chill mountaintop, freezing mists coat plants with rime ice.

2

Tidewater and Backwater

In 1609 the Reverend Robert Gray delivered a sermon to a tiny congregation drawn from the struggling infant colony of Virginia. Gray gave his blessing to the colony, but he also spoke words of doubt. In fact, as he discussed the American Indians of the region, he raised a "first objection" to the colony's very existence. "By what right or warrant," he asked, "can we enter into the land of these Savages, take away their rightfull inheritance from them, and plant ourselves in their places, being unwronged or unprovoked by them?"

To this day, Robert Gray's question remains unanswered. It tainted the heroism of America's drive from the Atlantic to the Pacific, from the first British efforts at commerce and conversion along the Virginia coast to the establishment of the final Indian reservation on a desolate expanse of the distant West. In the Border States, apparently, the question was never seriously considered. When the first white men settled there, red men of several great tribal stocks—Algonquian, Shawnee, Iroquoian—lived and hunted in the virgin forests

An antebellum Tidewater plantation is portrayed at left in a painting of the period. Besides the "big house," the anonymous painter depicted slave cabins, barns, a warehouse at the plantation's dock and a tobacco ship under full sail.

and rich valleys of the region. Of them all, only a single significant remnant survives today: the 4,500-odd Cherokees living in western North Carolina on the Qualla Reservation, adjoining the Great Smoky Mountains National Park.

The rest of the Border States' people are descendants of immigrants. There have been Africans, French, Germans, Swiss, Welsh, and—by far the largest number—English and Scotch-Irish.

Between 1607 and 1609, some subjects of King James I of England founded two successful "plantations" abroad. In the earlier year, a group of Englishmen struggled across the Atlantic to Virginia. In the latter, Scotsmen thrust across the Irish Sea to northern Ireland; subsequently, many of them would continue on to America. By the end of the century, and throughout the century to follow, the two groups were to meet in the Border States. Together, the English who came directly to the New World and their Scottish cousins who detoured by way of Ireland determined much of the course of American history. From the coastal Tidewater region, settled by the English, came the first great leaders of the new republic. From the high Appalachian Backwater region, dominated by the Scotch-Irish, came the first experience of the American west and an image of the westerner that has

Indians gather around a campfire in a 16th Century engraving of a water color by John White. White's paintings and drawings constitute a faithful record of early colonization on the Virginia and North Carolina coasts.

captured popular imagination around the world. To understand the Border States it is necessary to know these two groups of people and their turbulent histories.

The Tidewater, of course, proved to be the birthplace of the Border States and of the United States itself when the Jamestown Colony was founded there in 1607. But even Jamestown had significant forerunners, in Sir Walter Raleigh's two bold but unsuccessful attempts to colonize the coast of what is now North Carolina.

In 1585 Raleigh sent 108 men to Roanoke Island off the coast of "Virginia," named after the Virgin Queen, Elizabeth I. The group sojourned on the island for 10 months, then ingloriously hitched a ride back to England with the old sea dog Francis Drake, who was in the New World chasing Spaniards and gold for the Queen.

Undiscouraged, Sir Walter organized a more ambitious expedition two years later. The second group, led by John White, had only about 90 men —but it also included 17 women and nine children, suggesting a growing English awareness of what was necessary for the establishment of a permanent colony in an unknown land. Unfortunately, the planning of the expedition was less farsighted in other respects. The colonists arrived in Roanoke

in July 1587, too late to plant and harvest a crop that year. What was worse, they did not bring enough food and other stores to survive through the winter. In August John White set sail for England for fresh supplies. Behind him he left his daughter and an infant granddaughter, Virginia Dare, the first child to be born in America of English parents.

White assumed, of course, that he would return in time to save the tiny settlement, but as it happened he was unable to bring a cargo back until 1590. When he finally got there, he found that the Roanoke colonists had totally disappeared. They left no clue to their disappearance—or hardly any. Carved on a tree were the letters C R O; the gatepost of the palisade bore the one word CROATOAN, the name of an island and a tribe of Indians to the south. So the Lost Colony passed into legend. Massacred by Indians? Assimilated by the tribe and carried inland? Wiped out by hostile Spaniards? Lost at sea in a desperate attempt to return to England? The truth is still unknown.

Sir Walter Raleigh's failures in the New World lost him both fortune and favor. But the knowledge that had been gained helped provide the impetus for a new attempt—and, at last, a successful one. In 1607 the Virginia Company, a royally chartered but privately financed enterprise for colonization and trade, landed a new group of colonists well north of Roanoke Island, in the Chesapeake Bay Tidewater, now part of the state of Virginia. There, on a river called the James in honor of King James I, the 144 new arrivals founded the Jamestown Colony.

For years, the Jamestown colonists were plagued by disappointment and pursued by disaster. They started out by choosing the worst possible spot for their settlement: a marshy, mosquito-infested, poorly watered peninsula. Worse still, they were just the wrong sort of people to make their way in the wilderness. Too many of them were of the class then called gentlemen, unused to work of any kind; among the "craftsmen" they brought with them were a barber and a perfumer. And they had no intention of learning how to work. In their own view, they had come to discover gold, to explore a passage to the South Seas and to build "a great cittie," not to demean themselves by common labor. In the end, they found neither instant riches nor easy routes, and most of them filled graves rather than treasure chests.

Attacked by Indians from without, divided by internal quarrels and jealousies, the settlers had

The marriage in 1614 of the English colonist John Rolfe and Pocahontas, daughter of the native Indian chieftain Powhatan, reconciled the Indians and white men of the Jamestown area in a peace that was to last eight years. Two years after the wedding Rolfe took Pocahontas to England, where she was presented at the court of King James I with the courtesies due a princess. But the trip ended sadly: in less than a year Pocahontas sickened and died, and Rolfe returned to America alone.

to live on their fast-dwindling ship's stores. Occasionally they turned to the Indians, asking "those people which were our mortall enemies to releeve us with victuals, as Bread, Corne, Fish and Flesh." They themselves made little use of the teeming life in the waters and woods around them, for they were neither hunters nor fishermen.

It is not surprising that a company of men so inept began to die off almost from the start. Between June and the autumn of its first year, half the little colony died. They died, said one settler, from "cruell diseases, such as Swellings, Flixes, Burning Fevers, and by warres . . . but for the most part they died of meere famine."

For a moment in 1608 the gloom lifted when Captain John Smith became president of the colony council. No gentleman (his parents were tenant farmers on the estate of one Peregrine Bertie, Lord Willoughby), egotistical, given to exaggeration, Smith had lived as a soldier of fortune, serving in the armies of France, Holland and Transylvania. In the New World, as in the Old, his life was one of incredible adventure and hairbreadth escapes from death (the tale of his rescue by the Indian princess Pocahontas, once generally considered fiction, is now accepted as fact by most authorities). But the 27-year-old blusterer, with his bristling mustaches and iron armor, proved to be a natural leader and a stern realist.

As leader of the colony, he traded with friendly Indians and defended his settlement against unfriendly ones. The gentlemen under his command were forbidden to search for gold and put to planting corn instead. Most important of all, he spoke forthright common sense to his employers back in England. When the Virginia Company sent a note demanding that the colonists guarantee a profitable return on the company's investment, John Smith replied: "When you send againe I entreat you rather send but thirty Carpenters, husbandmen, gardiners, fishermen, blacksmiths, masons and diggers up of trees . . . than a thousand of such as we have; for except wee be able both to lodge them and feed them, the most will [waste away] with want of necessaries before they can be made good for anything."

Then darkness closed in again. In September 1608, a second group of colonists arrived—another group of useless gentlemen-adventurers, like the first. During the autumn of the following year an injury from a gunpowder explosion forced Smith to return to England, and the winter of 1609-1610 marked the low point of Jamestown's fortunes, the famous "Starving Time." Huddled in their fragile fort beside the river, the desperate colonists ate "doggs, catts, ratts, and snakes," boiled horsehides, and—in one instance—"salted wife." (The cannibal was duly executed.) Of the 500 men and women living in Jamestown in October, only 60 emaciated survivors greeted the spring.

Somehow, against all the odds, the colony struggled on. New shipments of men and supplies from England did little to strengthen its feeble grasp on life. But in 1614 a man named John Rolfe set Jamestown's security and prosperity on a firm basis. He, rather than John Smith, who usually gets the credit, may be regarded as the true founder of the Virginia colony.

Along with the other colonists, Rolfe had suffered the privations of the place and the time—and some others as well. He had set sail from England in 1609 with his wife. The journey was even harder than most; Rolfe's vessel was shipwrecked in the Bermudas, and his infant daughter, born in the islands, died there. The little party built two small ships and completed the voyage to Virginia, but Rolfe's young wife died soon afterward.

Then Rolfe's affairs took a turn for the better. In 1612 he began a series of experiments in tobacco raising, combining the bitter plant used by Virginia's Indians with strains of a milder type from the West Indies. Two years later he took a second wife: Pocahontas, the Indian maiden who as a girl had saved John Smith's life—and who was also the favorite daughter of Powhatan, the most powerful Indian chief in the vicinity. The marriage was a successful one, apparently inspired by love. It also had important consequences for the colony as a whole, for it ushered in an eight-year truce with the Indians, a period during which the Virginia colony grew strong and unified.

In that same year of 1614, John Rolfe sent his first shipment of improved Virginia tobacco to England—perhaps his most important contribution to the colony's welfare. Tobacco, brought to the mother country in the 1580s by Sir Walter Raleigh, had already become almost as controversial a subject as it is today. Indignant pamphleteers contemptuously termed it the "sot weed," and King James I thundered that smokers were "guilty of sinful and shameful lust." But the tobacco habit soon spread from the gentry to the common people; as one modern historian puts it, tobacco was "the bane of the moralists, but the poor man's luxury." And for Virginia, it truly proved to be a golden weed.

Low in bulk, high in value, tobacco was a staple crop that grew readily in Virginia's soil and climate, could be cultivated by unskilled labor and found a ready market abroad. What was more, John Rolfe had produced a strain of tobacco that proved enormously popular. Soon every clearing in the colony, and even parts of the streets of Jamestown itself, were planted in tobacco. By 1617, only three years after Rolfe's first shipment, Virginia was exporting nearly 20,000 pounds of tobacco annually. Tobacco actually became a form of currency, like gold or silver. In 1619, for example, when a subsidiary of the Virginia Company sent 90 young women as wives for the planters in exchange for the cost of their passage, the price was paid in tobacco.

But tobacco brought more than women to the New World: it also provided an incentive for able, land-hungry Englishmen to own their own farms, and thus changed the course of Virginia's history. In 1616 the Virginia Company agreed to grant 50 acres of land to any settler who paid his own passage across the Atlantic, with an additional 50 acres for each person he brought with him. Drawn by the offer, new arrivals pushed out along the James River and spread into the countryside.

The success of tobacco was not without its dangers. With alarming speed, Virginia was committing itself to a one-crop economy. Attempts by the King and the Virginia Company to impose acreage restrictions on tobacco and to encourage the growing of such crops as mulberries, hemp and flax failed to stem the tide of tobacco farming. For better or worse, the Virginia Tidewater was reaping the immediate benefits and incurring the future scourges of a single cash crop. The most sinister portent of that future came in August 1619, when John Rolfe noted that "a Dutch man-of-Warre" had put into Jamestown and sold "20 Negars" to the colonial government; the government in turn sold the Negroes to its citizens. It was the beginning of the slave trade in the United States.

Eventually, from their native plains and hills and villages, predominantly along the western coast of Africa, millions of black men and women would follow these first 20 to the Border States. They would come in bondage, torn from ancient roots, separated forever from their own past, to create a considerable portion of the wealth and culture of the Border States and the nation. Their labor would make possible the great tobacco, rice and cotton plantations of the South; their condition would one day incite a bloody civil war; and

A monument to the grandeur of the Virginia Tidewater, Westover was built in 1730 by William Byrd II. Beneath the plantation residence, designed in the style of a British Georgian manor house, are a secret room and a network of subterranean passages, presumably built as refuges from hostile Indians. In colonial days, ships from England sailed up the James River to Westover, bringing manufactured goods from the mother country and picking up cargoes of tobacco.

the consequences of the deep injustices wrought against them would persist, to torment the civic and moral peace of the region and the country.

Paradoxically, the same year that the Dutch ship left its unhappy cargo in Virginia, the first popularly elected legislative body in America—the House of Burgesses—met in Jamestown. Thus, in the same place and the same year, a nation-to-be carried on its first experiments in self-government and in chattel slavery. Taken together, the two experiments posed a contradiction that would eventually rend Virginia, the Border States and America asunder.

With tobacco as the economic foundation of the colony and self-determination becoming its chief principle, progress was steady. In 1624 King James dissolved the Virginia Company and made Virginia a crown colony. Its inhabitants included the descendants of those gentlemen-adventurers, laborers, convicts, homeless slum children, and women who had been sent to Jamestown over the years. Fresh migrations constantly brought free Englishmen ready to plant their own acres, accumulate their own capital and shape their own government. Some aspects of the world that they built for themselves can be seen today at Williamsburg, Virginia, which became the colonial capital

after Jamestown was destroyed by a fire in 1698.

The most famous restoration in America, Williamsburg is as authentic and complete a historical experience as research and money could combine to create. Visitors live again in a world of cobbled streets, taverns and small shops, dominated by the imposing Governor's Palace, the colonial capitol and the building designed by Christopher Wren for the College of William and Mary. In this setting Virginia's leaders received their early experience of government. George Washington, Patrick Henry, George Mason, Thomas Jefferson—the list extends to a roll call of early American history.

The shape and pattern of Tidewater society can be seen even more concretely in the mansions of the region, which rose in solitary elegance among woodlands, spacious lawns and cultivated fields. Here, far from the busy capital, life was regulated by the rhythm of the seasons and by the arrival of the tobacco ships in late fall or early winter. Sailing gracefully up the rivers, the ships docked at planters' private wharves to unload luxuries from the mother country and take on cargoes of tobacco.

The houses these ships visited were large but not ostentatious. While they incorporated the comforts and beauties that were the fruits of wealth, they were never designed for the display of wealth alone. (In this respect, they were precisely the opposite of the imitation châteaux and castles that a later, *nouveau riche,* society scattered across the United States.) Gentlemen farmers and merchants, managing their own affairs and the affairs of an infant nation, built these estates. They did not build them alone. By 1750 some 40 per cent of Virginia's people were slaves. Without them neither the rich fields nor the gracious houses would have come into existence.

When the French and Indian War broke out, owners of some of the Virginia mansions had to postpone their personal undertakings. George Washington was one of them. He left his work on Mount Vernon above the placid Potomac to go to the roiling headwaters in the west. He and others who would emerge as America's first military leaders during the Revolutionary War received their internship during this struggle, which formally lasted from 1754 until 1763. In Washington's leadership and the Americans' experiences with guerrilla fighting, in renewed awareness of the colonies' interdependence on each other and in their growing sense of independence from Britain, the French and Indian War was a prelude for the larger conflict soon to follow.

The French and Indian struggle also revealed beyond dispute that a new frontier was being forged beyond the mountains, in the Backwater country of the west. The largest number of its people were descendants of that other migration King James I had brought about in 1609, when he "planted" a colony of loyal Scotch Presbyterians in the six counties of northern Ireland. The men of this so-called "Ulster Plantation" were not expected to blend or merge with the native population; indeed, they were forbidden to marry Irishwomen. Their mission, as a modern historian has put it, was "to hold the wild Irish down and make Ireland Protestant."

For a time, the Ulster colony prospered. But James' successor, Charles I, virtually suppressed the Presbyterian religion of the Ulster Scots, and in 1666 a new king, Charles II, struck at their cattle trade by prohibiting the importation of beef into England and Scotland. Other English enactments ruined the Ulstermen's woolen trade and imposed heavy taxes and high rentals on lands they had built into productive farms. Stifled in their pursuit of both commerce and religion, the persecuted colonists desperately turned to America.

Between 1700 and 1730 some 20,000 of these Scotch-Irish came to the New World; by the mid-dle of the century they made up one quarter of the population of Pennsylvania. From there, they began to filter down through the Great Valley of the Appalachians, opening up the back country of Virginia and North Carolina. In smaller numbers, they penetrated inland from the Carolina coast.

After the French and Indian War, which came to an end in 1763, the Scotch-Irish flooded into North Carolina. Because of its treacherous coast, this colony, carved out of Virginia by Charles II in 1663, had not been settled directly from Europe but had drawn its people mainly from the overflow of neighboring colonies. Sometimes called "a valley of humility between two mountains of conceit," North Carolina never nurtured the aristocratic pretensions of Virginia or South Carolina. Now, with Highland Scots making their largest American settlement there and the Scotch-Irish settlers pouring in from Pennsylvania (and, to a lesser extent, from Virginia), the democratic character of the colony was firmly established.

Wherever they went, in fact, the Ulstermen had that effect. Settlers twice removed from their Scottish homeland, they exerted the second important influence on the Border States. As the English along the Tidewater sketched the outlines of the republic to be born, so the Scotch-Irish foreshadowed the character of men who kept the United States from remaining a seaboard nation. Theirs was a character that combined religious zeal with a devouring hunger for land and more land—it came to be said that the Scotch-Irish kept the Sabbath and everything else they could lay their hands on. Out of past persecution, in the words of the writer Constance Lindsay Skinner, there "emerged a type of man who was high-principled and narrow, strong and violent, as tenacious of his own rights as he was blind often to the rights of others, acquisitive yet self-sacrificing, but most of all fearless, confident of his own power, determined to have and to hold." And from their first forays into the Backwater country, these frontiersmen fought to take the land into the American fold.

Resourceful traders had already penetrated some of the mountain fastness of the back country. As early as 1671, for example, a Virginia merchant, Abraham Wood, had sent two agents westward from his trading post. Making the first recorded passage through the Appalachians, the men reached New River, a tributary of the Ohio; two years later, another team sent out by Wood traveled southwest across the present state of North Carolina, catching an early glimpse of the future routes to Tennessee and Kentucky. In the 18th Century, still other traders ventured farther and farther into the unknown land. Thus, in the spring of 1752, the trader-explorer Christopher Gist recorded a sojourn at "Wealin or Scalp Creek," the site of present-day Wheeling, West Virginia; and in the autumn of that year John Finley, a Pennsylvania trader, canoed down the Ohio River to the Great Falls of the Ohio, where Louisville, Kentucky, now stands.

It was in the last decades of the 18th Century, however, that the Scotch-Irish began to dominate the Backwater. It was then that one of the most remarkable groups of men to leave their stamp on the Border States first strode across the horizon. They were called the long hunters. For months and even years at a stretch they left their homes in the lowland settlements to explore the lonely wilderness. Following buffalo traces, Indian trails and their own instincts, they discovered the gaps in the towering mountain ranges and the passages through the seemingly impenetrable forests. Year after year, such men breached the mountain barriers and searched beyond, in the fabulous country of "Kaintuck." And close behind them there gathered a tide of settlers. By river and through the Cumberland Gap, these followers soon made their hazardous voyages to claim the rich canebrakes and green meadows of the waiting land.

To the long hunters fell the unrepeatable experience of seeing the Border States when the fields were alive with wildflowers and thundering hooves, the forests virgin, the waters clear and the skies filled with the throb of wings. Of all the men who had that experience, none was so renowned as Daniel Boone. Boone's own migrations were a microcosm of a larger pattern. Born in Pennsylvania in 1734, he traveled by covered wagon with his Quaker father and family down the Great Valley to the Yadkin River in western North Carolina. Then, restless and curious, a woodsman and a loner despite wife and children, he came to know the American west of his time as did no other man.

Boone's adventures took him as far south as St. Augustine, Florida, and as far west as Wyoming, but it was his leadership in the settlement of Kentucky that made him famous. He moved his own and other families from North Carolina to Kentucky, and led the party that cut the Wilderness Road through the Cumberland Gap into central Kentucky and thereby unlocked the west.

Yet Boone died owning little of the vast land he had mastered. His future, and the future of

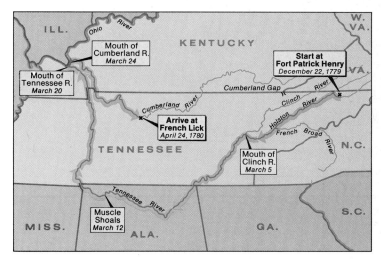

In the winter of 1779-1780, the Scotch-Irish pioneer John Donelson led some 300 settlers on a historic journey: a four-month, circuitous trip that opened up an all-water route from the Appalachians to central Tennessee. Beset by savage cold, treacherous shoals and hostile Indians, the group worked its way down the Holston and Tennessee Rivers from Fort Patrick Henry to Muscle Shoals. To get to their destination, a colony at French Lick, on the site of modern Nashville, the settlers floated 200 miles northwest to the Ohio River, then went upstream to the Cumberland and southeast to their goal.

settlers who came after him, was accurately predicted by an angry, pockmarked Cherokee chief, Dragging Canoe, on a March day in 1775. Dragging Canoe had gone to Sycamore Shoals on the banks of the Watauga River, there to deal in land with a company of white men led by the ambitious speculator Judge Richard Henderson. When negotiations were completed, the chief caught Daniel Boone's hand. "We have given you a fine land, Brother," he muttered, "but you will find it under a cloud and a dark and bloody ground."

The words forecast all the horrors soon to be endured in the struggling settlements and lonely frontier forts. No one on the "dark and bloody ground" remained untouched by cruelty and grief. Violent death at any age was such a common experience that one elderly woman told a traveler the most beautiful sight she had ever seen in Kentucky was a young man dying a natural death in his bed.

If settlers died, so did dreams. The life of Richard Henderson, who signed the treaty at Sycamore Shoals, is a saga of vaulting ambition and blasted hopes. In the North Carolina backwoods, Richard Henderson rose from constable and deputy sheriff to justice of the superior court —but his mind turned constantly to lands still farther west. As early as 1769 he sent Daniel Boone on an exploring journey into Kentucky and by 1773 he had conceived a fantastic plan for the development of the western wilderness.

Henderson's dream was nothing less than the creation of a 14th American colony, to be called Transylvania—and to be wholly owned by a company he himself had formed. At Sycamore Shoals, it seemed that the dream might become a reality. In exchange for a pledge of $10,000 in sterling, guns and provisions, the Cherokees handed over a domain of some 20 million acres, including most of the present state of Kentucky and a large tract in Tennessee. But this was in 1775—the eve of the American Revolution. Within a decade the power of the British government, which might have confirmed Henderson's claims, had vanished from the Backwater; in its place, there were the sovereign states of Virginia and North Carolina, which promptly annulled the Sycamore Shoals treaty. As recompense for the time and money he had spent, Henderson was granted some 200,000 acres between the Ohio and Green Rivers. Instead of a colony, he contented himself with a village.

Yet Henderson left his mark on the land that slipped so quickly out of his grasp. In 1775 he founded the first settlement in central Kentucky—Boonesborough, named after his faithful employee and friend Daniel Boone. And in 1779 he furthered the exploration of the region by sending two parties of settlers, one by land and one by water, to make the journey from the Watauga and Holston settlements, in present-day east Tennessee, to the French Lick (a salt outcrop discovered by French traders) on the distant Cumberland River, far to the west.

The overland group was led by a dogged Scotch-Irishman named James Robertson, the Indian agent for North Carolina and the head of the Watauga settlement. Driving its own herds of horses, cattle and sheep, the party set out in October. The pioneers crossed the mountains through the Cumberland Gap, followed an Indian trail called the Great Warrior's Path for a distance, then broke their own trail southwestward. On Christmas Day, 1779, they reached the French Lick; later, they crossed the ice-covered Cumberland to the site where the city of Nashville would eventually stand.

As for the second expedition, its journey was little less than incredible. From a point on the Holston River near the present-day city of Kingsport, Tennessee, some 30 flatboats floated down the Holston to the Tennessee River, down the full length of the Tennessee to the Ohio River, up the Ohio to the mouth of the Cumberland River, and up the Cumberland to the French Lick. It was a voyage of more than 900 miles (the direct overland distance is less than 240 miles). What was more, it was a voyage through a country almost entirely unexplored by white men.

In four months, the 300 men, women and children who embarked on the voyage experienced enough misery, sickness, terror and death to supply a whole school of novelists. Scotch-Irishman John Donelson, who led the flotilla in his flatboat *Adventure,* was an inept man, inexperienced in meeting the challenges of the frontier. There were delays due to ice in the rivers and days of hunger when the men had to forage for food; cold rains added to the suffering. Worst of all was the ever-present danger of ambush by Indians and of sudden death. One family, traveling on a boat with several friends, came down with smallpox; as a sort of quarantine, their boat was allowed to fall behind the others, only to be attacked by the Indians. While their companions ahead listened to their pitiful screams, 28 people were massacred.

The flotilla's survivors—among them John Donelson's 13-year-old daughter Rachel, who was to become the wife of Andrew Jackson—settled in the rich middle region of Tennessee. Among the passengers on the perilous inland voyage were a number of Negroes. As pioneers sought new lands and freedoms, they carried with them slaves to help insure the success of their ventures—not always (and not even often in the uplands, where land holdings were small), but often enough to establish slavery throughout the Border States. Thus, the paradox of a passion for freedom combined with a practice of maintaining slavery was etched ever more deeply on the conscience of the settlers.

In a sense, the agony endured by that first beachhead at Jamestown, back in 1607, was repeated in all the little enclaves of white settlement that spread across the interior reaches of the Border States. From the Tidewater to the Backwater, from landed gentry to long hunters, America was on its way. Painfully but irrevocably, it was cutting its umbilical cord with England. In the Tidewater, for a time, men might continue to look back across the ocean that linked them with their past and the places of their heritage. In the back country, men could look only as far as the mountain walls that surrounded them—until they turned and gazed to the west, and a new heritage.

Daniel Boone points toward the Bluegrass country in this romanticized painting of the moment on June 7, 1769, when for the first time he "saw with pleasure the beautiful level of Kentucky." Four of his five hunting companions returned home that winter (the fifth was killed by Indians), but Boone wandered through Kentucky until 1771 before returning to North Carolina with tales of a "second paradise."

The "Eden of the West"

By the middle of the 18th Century, fur traders and hunters began to spread the word of a fabulous "Eden of the West" lying beyond the Appalachian border of colonial America. In the frontier settlements of Virginia and North Carolina, men like Daniel Boone (above) preached the gospel of Kentucky, with its "myriads of trees, some gay with blossoms, others rich with fruits," where "buffalo were more frequent than cattle in the settlements."

In 1775 Boone guided a group of settlers through the Cumberland Gap, a natural opening in the towering Appalachian barrier that led to the easiest overland route to Kentucky. They were soon followed by thousands of pioneers, like the ones shown in the 19th Century engravings on these pages. In the lush Bluegrass country, the pioneers cleared ancient forests, built log cabins, fought off Indians and became part of a tradition that lives on in the American spirit long after the disappearance of the frontier.

THE TRADER WHO LEARNED THE SECRET OF CUMBERLAND GAP

John Finley, a fur trader in the Ohio Valley, first saw Kentucky's rich Bluegrass country in 1752, when he was taken there as a captive of the Shawnee tribe. He learned from his captors that the area could be reached fairly easily from the Cumberland Gap by following an old warpath, and in 1769 he guided Daniel Boone's party of long hunters over this Indian route to the Kentucky River.

Lonely pathfinders on the long hunt

The first white men to explore Kentucky in the mid-18th Century were buckskin-clad frontiersmen who came from settlements on the eastern slopes of the Appalachians. Such men traveled alone for hundreds of miles to map claims for land speculators and to trade with the Indians. Soon they were joined by sharpshooting long hunters, drawn from frontier farms each fall by the promise of a rich harvest of furs in "Kaintuck." The long hunts lasted for months, even years, as the adventurers tracked buffalo, elk, deer and bear across the vast hunting lands of the Cherokee and Shawnee tribes. Indian attacks were common and caches of fur were vulnerable to Indian plunderers—a peril of the hunt mirrored in the words carved on a tree trunk by one anguished hunter: "2300 deerskins lost. Ruination, by God." Worst of all was the risk of capture and torture *(bottom, right)*.

But the long hunters persisted—and they learned the land. The information they brought back across the mountains provided both impetus and guidance for the great western migration. Christopher Gist *(below)* singlehandedly mapped most of northeastern Kentucky. John Finley *(left)* anticipated Daniel Boone *(top, right)* in seeking and finding an overland route to the prized Bluegrass country of central Kentucky. Each contributed a vital link in a chain of discoveries that opened the way to Kentucky for a flood of settlers.

THE FIRST SURVEYOR IN KENTUCKY

Christopher Gist, who made the first accurate survey of northeastern Kentucky, braves the Appalachians on his return home to North Carolina in 1751. The educated son of one of Baltimore's founders, Gist rejected city comforts for the rugged frontier life.

DANIEL BOONE AND HIS "BEST FREN"

In the hands of skilled long hunters like Daniel Boone *(right)*, the legendary Kentucky rifle was the fastest and most accurate weapon of its time. Frontiersmen took great pride in their rifles; Boone carved frontier scenes, his initials and the words "Best Fren" on opposite sides of the stock of his rifle "Ticklicker," which probably got its name from Boone's boast that he could "flick a tick off a bar's back at a hundred paces." This long rifle—its barrel was 46 inches long— was built originally as a small-bore .29-caliber weapon in order to reduce the size and weight of the lead bullets Boone had to carry. It was gradually enlarged over the years by reboring to its final .41-caliber size. Like all flintlock rifles, it was muzzle-loaded with powder and a bullet rammed down with a light wooden ramrod carried under the barrel. A tallow-soaked cloth, placed under the bullet, facilitated swift loading. To fire the rifle, a small priming charge of gunpowder was poured from the powder horn into the flintlock and then ignited by a spark.

THE FRONTIERSMAN WHO WAS TOO TOUGH TO KILL

The ordeal of Simon Kenton, captured by Indians in 1778, illustrates the stubborn toughness of the Kentucky frontiersman. After being driven through the woods tied to the bare back of a wild colt *(above)*, Kenton was displayed in Indian villages throughout Ohio and repeatedly forced to run the gauntlet between rows of club-swinging Indians. Three times reprieved from death at the stake, he eventually escaped and made his way back to Kentucky.

THE WILDERNESS ROAD TO BOONESBOROUGH

Camping along the Wilderness Road on a winter night, a migrating family prepares a meal under the canopy of a pine forest. Many pioneers chose to travel the rough road in winter, when they could use boatlike sledges to haul their goods over the snow-covered ground.

Boone's Fort, built in 1775, was the main structure of Boonesborough. Intended as a place of refuge during Indian attacks, the fort withstood a 10-day siege in 1778. Later, as the Wilderness Road's terminus, it became a stopover for settlers heading deeper into Kentucky.

Crude flatboats, like those shown here, drifted down the Ohio River in a steady stream after the end of the Revolutionary War, carrying entire families and their possessions. The river itself was the only source of power; the long "sweeps" at either end of a flatboat served as rudders to keep the boat in the channel until it was finally run aground at a choice spot. Once ashore, the flatboat often served as a temporary home before being broken up for building materials.

A FLATBOAT PILGRIMAGE
DOWN THE OHIO RIVER

Alternate routes to the new frontier

In the last quarter of the 18th Century, settlers took two routes to Kentucky. Most early settlers followed Daniel Boone's Wilderness Road *(top, left)* for about 150 miles from the Cumberland Gap to the Bluegrass country. At the end of the road lay Boonesborough *(bottom, left),* where the weary pioneers, after weeks of living on venison and wild turkey, often begged for a slice of bread. They soon left Boonesborough for the unclaimed land in the beckoning Bluegrass vista on the far side of the Kentucky River. By the mid-1780s, just after the Revolutionary War, there were already about 30,000 settlers in Kentucky. With the cessation of British-supported Indian raids along the Ohio River, that waterway increasingly rivaled the Wilderness Road as a route west. Flatboats descending the Ohio from Pittsburgh brought a new wave of settlers from the east, and by 1800 the new state of Kentucky boasted a population of 220,995.

A new log cabin begins to take shape as a settler and his neighbors fit foundation logs onto their proper notches. These builders are erecting an elaborate version of the familiar, windowless cabin in the background, typical of thousands that served as the first homes for generations of pioneers.

THE BEGINNING OF A SETTLER'S CABIN

An interior view of a well-finished log cabin shows how its undivided space was used by a frontier family. The beds were for parents, older children and guests. Younger children slept on pallets in the loft. The space around the fireplace served as a combination kitchen, workshop, and dining and living area.

AN ENTIRE FAMILY IN A SINGLE ROOM

A COZY HOMESTEAD
ON THE OLD FRONTIER

The typical settler's homestead shown in this picture contains a large log house and a smaller log cabin that may have been the original home on the site. Both buildings are roofed with closely fitted rows of wooden boards. A simple "worm" fence, requiring no posts, prevents cattle from wandering out of the clearing. Most frontiersmen were notoriously poor farmers; the fine stand of corn behind the clearing may be an artist's exaggeration of the tiny patch that was usually planted.

The little log cabin in the wilderness

When he had found and paced off his claim, a settler's first task was to build some sort of shelter quickly and cheaply from the materials at hand. In heavily wooded Kentucky the answer was the log cabin, the simple, utilitarian structure that was to become a romanticized symbol of frontier living. The earliest log cabins were crude, windowless affairs, barely the size of an average modern room, with chimneys made of mud and sticks and roofs of brush or rough boards. As settlements grew, however, larger one-room cabins could be built with community help. Neighbors for miles around could be counted on for a "log raisin'." It took only one day to cut the 70 or 80 logs that were needed and to build a rough log foundation. The second day was devoted to the organized musclework of "rolling up" the walls. The logs, usually 15 to 25 feet long, were rolled up inclined poles on opposite walls and fitted onto the notched ends of the logs at right angles to them. In this fashion, all four walls went up together. A third day was required to finish the roof and the floor, fill in the cracks with mud and moss, and install a heavy, barred door. The cabin completed, the host plied his neighbors with as much food and whiskey as they could hold. In later years the log cabin gave way to the more spacious two- or three-room log house. Then the cabin, having outlived its usefulness, either became a lowly outbuilding or was destroyed.

The abduction of Daniel Boone's daughter Jemima and two friends by Shawnees in 1776 led to a spirited chase and rescue. The rescuers quickly claimed two girls as brides.

Wielding an ax in 1787, Mrs. John Merrill killed four redskins as they came through the smashed door, then finished off two more who tried to come down the chimney.

The "flower" of Kentucky womanhood

The women of Bryant's Station, pretending not to notice Indians lying in ambush, risked their lives to draw water from a spring outside the walls during a siege in 1782.

A heroine of old Kentucky, Mrs. Samuel Daviess surprised a bandit who invaded her home in 1783. Only the year before, Mrs. Daviess had survived kidnapping by Indians.

There was nothing frail or dainty about the women who helped to settle Kentucky. As handy with an ax and long rifle as with a spinning wheel and loom, they cleared forests, built cabins, worked in the fields, cared for the sick, and defended themselves against both Indians and white desperadoes. Above and beyond these tasks, they were also expected to bear children and lots of them, for large families meant more hands to share the farm work. ("A numerous family is the most prosperous cattle we can raise in these woods," said one astute pioneer.) It was not unusual for a woman to marry at 16, have six to eight children by the age of 30 and be a wornout grandmother in her forties.

Competition for the heavily outnumbered single girls was brisk, but marriage laws were only casually observed. Common-law marriages were frequent in settlements where no clergyman was present to formalize the ceremony. Abandonment and bigamy also occurred; when Daniel Boone returned to Boonesborough in 1778 after being held captive by Indians for a bare four months, he found that his wife had returned to North Carolina and remarried. According to Boone's memoirs, he got her back after "a series of difficulties, an account of which would swell a volume."

A CIRCUIT RIDER MAKES HIS ROUNDS

Traveling through roadless country on horseback, a circuit rider might spend a month or more on a route that extended over 400 miles. The first riders were often Methodists, but after 1780 they were joined by preachers of other denominations—many of them self-appointed.

Carrying the Gospel to the frontier

Hard on the heels of the Kentucky pioneers came circuit riders like the one above, itinerant preachers who carried not only the word of God, but also books, letters and medicines to the distant corners of the frontier. These dedicated missionaries rode from one settlement to another, visiting with the families along their route during the week and preaching at a central point on Sunday. The circuit riders often conducted their simple meetings outdoors. They welcomed all comers regardless of church affiliation, and the meetings were among the earliest social gatherings in the wilderness. While children played and picnicked at the edges of the meeting grounds, parents were urged to repent their sins and pray for forgiveness, lest they face the wrath of an angry God.

The informality of these revival meetings, and their stress on personal religious experience rather than church ritual, made them especially appealing to the settlers, few of whom were members of organized churches. In 1801 a mass revival meeting at Cane Ridge, Kentucky, attracted 20,000 people. Such huge gatherings developed into a frontier institution, the annual four-day camp meeting (right), one of the most important religious and social events in pioneer family life.

EVENING SERVICE AT
A KENTUCKY CAMP MEETING

In flickering firelight a preacher exhorts his listeners during a night session of a 19th Century Kentucky camp meeting. Such camp meetings, which lasted several days, drew people from hundreds of miles around. Many moved their families into cabins ringing the grounds. Preachers worked in relays night and day to keep up a continuous barrage of inspiration, studded with quotations from the Scriptures and punctuated by hymns that were often adapted from popular ballads and sea chanteys. Enraptured listeners, encouraged to "let the spirit take them," frequently leaped, shouted and even went into convulsions. Those who fainted were gently laid out in an enclosure called the "glory pen." But camp meetings served a social as well as a religious function, giving old friends a chance to get together for a chat *(foreground)*. Long after churches took over the religious work of the camp meetings, the camp grounds continued to be meeting places.

3

High-spirited Politics

et us, then, fellow citizens, unite with one heart and one mind. . . . We are all republicans— we are Federalists," said Thomas Jefferson of Virginia in 1801. About a century and a half after that lofty appeal to patriotism, boss Edward Hull Crump of Tennessee had this to say about a political opponent: "In the art galleries of Paris there are 27 pictures of Judas Iscariot—none look alike but all resemble Gordon Browning; . . . neither his head, heart nor hand can be trusted; . . . he would milk his neighbor's cow through a crack in the fence." In every generation, from the time of Thomas Jefferson to the time of boss Ed Crump, both tones of voice, both modes of discourse, have constantly been heard in the Border States. The region's political life has alternated between statesmanship and showmanship. It has been noble and ignominious, lively and deadly; an art, a sport and a science. Its leaders have included philosophical giants and unlettered frontiersmen, lonely idealists and party-machine manipulators, ruthless reformers and tenacious defenders of the

Embarking on a bumpy roller coaster ride, E. H. "Boss" Crump beams for his supporters at an outing held in 1946. For more than 40 years the iron-fisted boss of a political machine based in Memphis, Tennessee, Crump died in 1954 at the age of 80.

status quo. Their campaigns, like their characters, have been fierce and humorous, loyal and vicious, always intense, and seldom guilty of the unpardonable sin of dullness.

Perhaps more than any other segment of life in the Border States, politics has both formed and reflected the character of the region—and the nation. The political system has produced a wide variety of heroes and knaves. By looking at them, we can grasp some of the key features of the system —a system that has been remarkably successful (32 of the first 36 years of the United States were spent under the Administrations of Virginian Presidents; of the 17 Presidents who held office up to the Reconstruction era, 11 were either born in or elected from the Border States) .

Political leaders from the Border States drew up the Declaration of Independence, the Bill of Rights and the Monroe Doctrine; but the region is also the birthplace of some of the most outlandish political practices ever seen in the United States. And these practices have been consistent, from colonial times down to the present day.

Diverse influences have combined to form the politics of the Border States. There has been the influence of the land and of a predominantly rural way of life. There has been a strain of violence in political life, yet political campaigns have been leavened by humor and high spirits—and often lubricated by spirits of another kind. Family connections have always been important in Border States politics, yet the political scene has been repeatedly dominated by towering individualists.

Of all these influences, the first mentioned—the rural nature of the region—was also the earliest to appear. Hunger for land had driven thousands of desperate Europeans across the Atlantic, and land was the earliest yardstick by which character and wealth were measured. As the most accessible and fertile acres were occupied, thousands of settlers pushed inland from the coast and down the Appalachian valleys from the north. They plodded over tortuous trails, faced the hardships of weather and wilderness, and risked death by tomahawk. They fought the French and the English; and they fought each other, when some of them formed unscrupulous land companies and sought, often by bribery or outright fraud, to take over enormous tracts and keep out the small settlers.

What they did *not* do was plant great cities in their region. Except for a few small communities along the seaboard and the main river arteries, the Border States remained a vast expanse of woods broken by occasional plantations and yeoman farms. In the census of 1790, only one site in the Border States—Richmond, Virginia—was classed as urban. In 1810 the three leading centers of population in the region were Richmond, with just 9,735 persons; Petersburg, Virginia, with only 5,668; and Louisville, Kentucky, with 1,357. Even by the time of the Civil War, no city in the region had reached a population of 25,000 and not a single town in North Carolina had as many as 10,000 inhabitants. As late as 1900, only four of the nation's 50 largest cities were in the Border States: Louisville ranked 18th in size; Memphis, 37th; Richmond, 46th; and Nashville, 47th.

In a nation on its way to becoming the urban and industrial colossus of the world, the people of the Border States persisted, until quite recently, much as they had begun: intensely rural in their economic life, their politics and their attitudes. In this course, they were supported by the philosophies and actions of their earliest leaders. These men, who exerted a lasting influence on our national structure, considered themselves, above all else, landed gentlemen. George Mason, who composed the Bill of Rights and waged a brilliant battle for its inclusion in the Constitution, was the owner and planter of the 5,000-acre Gunston Hall

estate. James Madison was, in Thomas Jefferson's opinion, Virginia's best farmer. John Marshall, the influential Chief Justice of the young United States, was known to his neighbors as the first president of the earliest Virginia agricultural society.

"Those who labour in the earth are the chosen people of God," Thomas Jefferson once declared; this philosopher, inventor, educator and statesman also confessed that "No occupation is so delightful to me as the culture of the earth." And Jefferson made sure that he had an ample amount of that earth to cultivate: at the age of 14 he inherited 2,750 acres, and over the years he gradually increased his holdings to 10,000 acres. By rotating crops, combating soil erosion and inventing new farming machinery, he proved himself as imaginative in agriculture as he was in government.

To men like Mason, Madison, Marshall and Jefferson, land meant more than material wealth. It was a way of life providing a base for responsible leadership. Of all the Virginian statesmen-farmers, George Washington towers as the prime example, and what is most exemplary about him is the way in which his career as a gentleman farmer flowered into a variety of other pursuits—surveyor of the western wilderness, political leader before the Revolution, commander of the Continental Army, first President of the United States.

When Washington purchased Mt. Vernon in 1754, the house was run-down and the holdings included exactly 2,126 acres. When he died in December 1799 (after inspecting a corner of his estate in a cold rain mixed with hail and snow), the serene and spacious mansion appeared much as it does today and the land comprised more than 8,000 acres. More than 200 people were required to maintain the house and work the fields. The nature of such a Virginia plantation—a community in itself—almost inevitably gave Washington a sense of pride laced with responsibility, the experience of command tempered by an awareness of the crosscurrents of human nature.

From Mt. Vernon, Washington went in 1759 to serve in the Virginia House of Burgesses, in 1775 to assume command of the Continental Army and in 1789 to become President of the new United States. In all these posts, he displayed the qualities most highly regarded in a rural society: practicality, physical strength (he could crush a walnut between his fingers) and passion (Gilbert Stuart, who painted the impassive portrait that has perpetuated a partially false image of Washington's nature, said that "All his features were indicative

On their way to fight the British at King's Mountain in 1780, backwoodsmen gather at the shore of Tennessee's Watauga River in the Great Smoky Mountains. *The Departure for King's Mountain,* by Tennessee-born painter Lloyd Branson, depicts John Sevier, on horseback at right, shaking hands with one of his officers. The battle, in which Sevier's frontiersmen defeated crack British troops, played a vital part in the drive for American independence.

of the most ungovernable passions, and had he been born in the forest he would have been the fiercest man among the savage tribes").

The Washington who lived as a proud, well-dressed, genteel landowner is to be encountered at Mt. Vernon. Another side of the man may be envisioned at a site 150 miles away, a quiet place called Valley Forge. There the winds and snows of winter still sweep down in cruel assault, as they did during the harsh testing time of 1777-1778, when Washington's patience, fortitude and charisma of command were put to a life-and-death trial —and proved equal to the needs of his ragged army and his unfledged country. At Valley Forge all that was most enduring in the rural tradition of the Border States proved itself triumphantly.

There was also another aspect of the land—the western waters—in which Washington was deeply involved. As a young surveyor and a soldier in the French and Indian War, he came to know intimately, as few of his planter peers did, the wide rivers and forests, the rich meadows and upthrust mountains, the abundant soil of the country stretching beyond the Tidewater and the Piedmont to the distant horizon. Eventually, Washington was to own some 45,000 acres of land west of the Allegheny Mountains. (Most of this western

land came to him for his services in the French and Indian War and through his purchases of the claims of fellow soldiers.)

As a statesman, then, Washington had firsthand experience of the whole rural spectrum in the Border States, from the pleasant life of the landed gentry to the free-for-all of the westward-moving frontier. He understood the new country—and it understood him. Within the aloof, bewigged English gentleman who as President considered taking the title of "High Mightiness" for himself, there existed the frontier American who could reassure an old Revolutionary War soldier that he still answered to the title of "Old Hoss."

Washington handsomely fulfilled another qualification for political leadership in the Border States, a quality just as important as a connection with the soil: the need for a man to be a fighter—and a winner. Among the men he led, demonstrations of physical courage or moral fortitude were respected and remembered—and Washington provided superb demonstrations of such courage and fortitude. At Fort Duquesne, for example, when he served in the French and Indian War, Washington rose from a sickbed to join in the fighting; in the battle, four bullets ripped through his coat.

But though the contentious, fractious nature

Clad in their Sunday best—and carrying their "shooting irons"
—members of the Hatfield clan pose for their picture in Logan
County, West Virginia, on the Kentucky border. For more
than 30 years the Hatfields fought a feud with the McCoys,
who lived in Kentucky, across the Big Sandy River. As many
as 200 people may have been killed in the long vendetta.

of a people who guarded their independence with
prickly jealousy was given heroic outlet in time of
war, it was sometimes reduced to petty ferocity in
the politics of peacetime. In North Carolina, particularly, there were duels. Between 1800 and 1860
at least 27 political duels in the state involved
legislators, governors or United States senators. In
Kentucky Henry Clay defended his Jeffersonian
Republicanism with dueling pistols against a fellow legislator who was a Federalist.

Elsewhere, in Kentucky and West Virginia especially, there were feuds. The most famous pitted
the Democratic Hatfields of West Virginia against
the Republican McCoys on the Kentucky side of
the Big Sandy River. The original causes of the
feud are lost in obscurity, but its subsequent ferocity has made it a symbol of unrelenting clan warfare. Between 1873 and 1890 murders, raids and
ambushes killed an unknown number of each
family—three McCoys died in a single encounter.
The courts were reluctant to involve themselves in
this tribal warfare and no aspect of local economy,
politics, education or social life was left unscarred
by the long, wasteful bloodbath.

In wartime the residents of the Border States
often proved to be mighty warriors but poor soldiers. They did not flinch from fighting, but they
did not always adapt well to the regimentation of
formal military service. For the most part, they
opposed large standing armies and made fighting
a highly personal affair that could easily extend
into political affairs. One of their typical figures
was the political leader and sometime soldier John
Sevier.

If George Washington stood for the world of
the Virginia Tidewater, John Sevier stood for the
land beyond the mountains. Sevier was among the
first of the authentic western heroes. Half English,
half French Huguenot, he combined the hard
muscles of an outdoorsman with the graceful manners of a courtier. He was not tall—five feet nine—
but he was lithe, and the sparkle of his dark blue
eyes softened the severity of his aquiline Roman
nose. J.G.M. Ramsey, one of Tennessee's earliest
historians, left a portrait of the man: "He was
fluent, colloquial, and gallant—frolicsome, generous and convivial—well informed, rather than well
read. Of books he knew little. Men, he had studied
well and accurately."

Sevier was born and reared in the Shenandoah
Valley, where in 1764, at the age of 19, he laid out
the town of New Market.

Married twice—first when he was 16, and next
to a girl who fell into his arms when she climbed
a stockade in flight from pursuing Indians—he had
18 children. His career as a Backwater frontiersman began in 1773, when he explored the Holston
and Watauga country and moved his wife and children, his parents and brothers and their families,
to the country that is now part of east Tennessee.

From the start of his life in the west, Sevier took
the lead in subduing the hostile Indians of the
hills and forests. In 1783 he built a home beside
the Nolichucky River where he lived while carrying the Indian war into the Cherokee country.
Sevier's exploits as an Indian fighter were tri-
umphs of both the bravery and brutality of the
frontier. He became especially famous for carrying
the fight to the Indians wherever he could find
them, rather than fighting from fortified stock-
ades. With the war cry "Here they are! Come on,
boys!", Sevier won the hatred and the grudging
admiration of the Cherokee and the devotion of
the back-country dwellers. The victory that won
him national honor, however, was the Battle of
King's Mountain in the American Revolution.

The Revolutionary War in the South had come
to a low ebb in the summer of 1780. Charleston
had fallen and the British general Lord Cornwallis
had launched a campaign to invade North Caro-

lina and cut Washington off from the Southern colonies. When Cornwallis marched without opposition north to Charlotte, North Carolina, it appeared that the British move to conquer North Carolina would prove successful. Cornwallis was uneasy about the back country, however, and sent a corps under one of his ablest officers, Major Patrick Ferguson, to organize Loyalist volunteers and quell rebellious forces in the interior.

Immediately, the settlers in the west decided to adopt Sevier's tactic of carrying the attack to the enemy. Unattached to any state militia or to the Continental Army, they shouldered their rifles, rendezvoused at the Sycamore Shoals of Watauga River, and set off across the Blue Ridge on the morning of September 26. It was all very informal and intense. Along the way the citizen-soldiers were joined by other volunteers and chose their leaders for four assaulting columns: Sevier, William Campbell, Isaac Shelby and Benjamin Cleveland. Their spirit was perfectly expressed in the command Cleveland gave his men just before the battle: "When you are engaged, you are not to wait for any word of command from me. I will show you, by example, how to fight; I can undertake no more. Every man must consider himself an officer, and act from his own judgment."

Patrick Ferguson and the splendidly uniformed and superbly equipped soldiers of the King took their stand on a low ridge called King's Mountain, about a mile and a half south of the North Carolina border. On the afternoon of October 7, in a drenching rain, the Backwater men reached the woods at its base. Soon afterward, the clouds lifted and there was sunshine as the patriots started on foot up the steep slopes surrounding the hilltop.

The Americans fought in Indian fashion, using the trees for cover. The British soldiers, exposed and in formation, mounted bayonet charges that were futile in the face of the accurate marksmanship of woodsmen, who could pick them off from all sides. Major Ferguson, blowing a silver whistle, indifferent to danger while two horses were shot from under him, rode along his line spurring his men on until he fell, mortally wounded. In a battle that lasted about an hour, the British forces were completely routed.

Thus a band of untrained frontiersmen, under the control of neither a state nor the Continental government, had dealt a stunning blow against trained English soldiers. Their victory rekindled the hopes of Americans everywhere, and Cornwallis fled back to South Carolina. Later, the

As rival candidates for the governorship of Tennessee, the Taylor brothers, Democrat Bob *(left)* and Republican Alf *(right),* entertain the voters with some country fiddlin' in this 1886 drawing. Bob won the election, but both men eventually served as governor and in Congress, displaying a home-spun humor that has become a tradition in Tennessee politics.

American general Nathanael Greene lured him on a costly pursuit across the Piedmont. (In March, 1781, when Cornwallis defeated Greene at the Battle of Guilford Courthouse, British losses were so great that the caustic man of letters Horace Walpole, back in England, remarked: "Lord Cornwallis has conquered his troops out of shoes and provisions, and himself out of troops.") Eventually, hemmed in at Yorktown, Virginia, Cornwallis surrendered to Washington. The date was October 19, 1781, almost exactly a year after the battle at King's Mountain.

George Washington called the dramatic encounter at King's Mountain a "proof of the spirit and resources of the country." Thomas Jefferson summarized its significance when he said, "It was the joyful annunciation of that turn of the tide of success which terminated the Revolutionary War with the seal of our independence." Even the British, who had denounced the "barbarian squirrel hunters" at King's Mountain as mongrels and the dregs of humanity, eventually came to the same conclusion. In the rolling periods of the time, Sir Henry Clinton, commander in chief of the British forces, was to write that the Battle of King's Mountain "proved the first Link of a Chain of Evils that followed each other in regular Succession until they at last ended in the total Loss of America." In a more local sense, it demonstrated the scrappiness and daring that have come to be hallmarks of the Border States.

Sevier returned home from King's Mountain, his popularity at a new height, and resumed his defense of the western settlements and his career in politics. When Kentucky was admitted to the Union in 1792 and Tennessee in 1796, it was, as historian Archibald Henderson has said, a "testimony of the martial instincts and unwavering loyalty of the transmontane people" that the two men chosen to lead their first state governments were Isaac Shelby in Kentucky and John Sevier in Tennessee. By the time of his death in 1815, Sevier had served Tennessee six times as governor and three times as representative to Congress.

It was inevitable that John Sevier would be a political as well as a military leader, for he had studied men too "well and accurately" not to win them over at the ballot box as he had won them over on the battlefield. He rode out to meet conflict head on and understood the popular mind of the Border States as did few others of his time. He did not have to learn—as did George Washington, for one—that success on election day depended on a variety of ingredients, not all of them impeccably high-minded. One ingredient was whiskey.

"Swilling the planters with bumbo"—that is, with alcoholic drinks—was the way one Tidewater citizen described the dispensing of free refreshments on election day. When George Washington ran for the House of Burgesses in 1755, he was defeated. He ran again in 1757, with the same result. But in the election of 1758 he adopted a new tactic: his agent supplied 391 voters and "unnumbered hangers-on" with 160 gallons of rum, wine, beer and cider—more than a quart and a half for each voter. It was characteristic that when he paid the bill for these beverages, Washington wrote, "I hope no exception were taken to any that voted against me but that all were alike treated and all had enough; it is what I much desired." Steeped in the ways of hospitality (many years later, after he returned to Mt. Vernon from the Presidency, he wrote that he and Martha were having dinner alone for the first time in 20 years), Washington sounded more like a host than a politician. But he won the 1758 election.

Even those who deplored the "low practices" of "treating"—among them Thomas Jefferson and James Madison—were forced to participate or lose at the polls. And not everyone condemned the practice. It has been argued by the historian C. S. Sydnor that "bountiful supplies of free liquor were responsible for much rowdiness, fighting, and drunkenness, but the fun and excitement of an election and the prospect of plentiful refreshments of the kind customarily consumed in that day helped to bring the voters to the polls. Thus in a perverse kind of way treating made something of a contribution to 18th Century democracy."

In North Carolina and Kentucky as well as in Virginia, election day became one of the chief public holidays. In 1811, a doctor in Edgecombe County, North Carolina, described electioneering as "a certain peculiar shake of the hand, called by our farmers the electioneering shake," and "purchasing brandy and drinking with the people." Fourteen years later another North Carolinian said he had won an election with the help of "white ruin [liquor], melons, and gingerbread." And as recently as 1955, when Wix Unthank became the first Democrat in many years to hold the office of county judge in Harlan County, Kentucky, his election was generally attributed to "Whiskey, Wedlock, and Workers."

The trio of "Ws" includes another important ingredient of Border States politics that dates back to the earliest days: the significance of a candidate's family. A political scientist, John Fenton, pointed out that in the Unthank election, "by 'wedlock' observers had reference to the importance of the family in local politics. Traditionally there are some four or five well-to-do and/or prolific Harlan families which rule the country. Unthank belongs to one of these families and his wife to another. Therefore, in both the primary and general election the two families united in support of his candidacy."

In 18th Century Virginia, it was virtually impossible to enter politics without belonging to one of the landed families. The first step of a budding statesman was to serve on the county court where, under the guidance of relatives and neighbors, he was broken in through a sort of apprenticeship. From this grassroots view of life he went on to the House of Burgesses, which was, of course, made up of gentlemen, a good many perhaps related to him. The entry of Virginia into the Union merely broadened the political horizon: after service in the state legislature, a man thus solidly grounded might become candidate for governor, representative or senator.

Strong family ties are characteristic of most rural people, but Kentuckians may have established something of a record for nepotism—or, in the local euphemism, assistance for some office-holder's kinfolks who need "looking after." The practice of placing wives, daughters, brothers, cousins and nephews on the public payroll has prevailed down to the present day.

The fact that the boundaries of kinship have often seemed limitless, extending to cousins many times removed, has multiplied the problem. At one time, for example, a certain Oscar Haggin wanted to be jailer for Breathitt County, Kentucky. He ran an announcement in the county seat newspaper, in which he stated: "Among those to whom I am related by blood or marriage are the following families: Bachs, Lovelys, Allens, McQuinns, Pattons, Landrums, Stampers, Watts, Watkins, Manus, Crafts, Calhouns, and the Nichols. My wife was a Crawford which makes our relation to the Jetts, Johnsons, Combs, Griffiths, Terrys, Amburgys, Bowmans, Heralds, Spences, Lawsons, Capes, Hargises, Days, Haddixes and Evans and many more." (Perhaps the chief difference between this appeal to relatives and the older, aristocratic Virginia dependence on family was that Haggin had to publish his genealogy. It would have been unnecessary in the world of the Lees, Randolphs, Fitzhughs and Washingtons.)

Family involvement in politics led to at least one good-natured conflict in the Border States, when the Taylor brothers waged their folksy, serio-comic War of the Roses during Tennessee's gubernatorial race of 1886. In a series of 41 debates, Robert L. Taylor, Democrat, and Alfred A. Taylor, Republican, traveled together throughout the state, stayed at the same hotels, spoke from the same platforms, and fought with wit, oratory, music and serious discussions of issues (in descending order of importance) to beat each other to the governor's chair. The Taylors were members of an old east Tennessee family. When one of them said they were "two roses from the same garden," their contest was promptly labeled the War of the Roses, and Alf adopted the red rose of Lancaster while Bob wore the white rose of York.

During the hard years of adjustment between the Reconstruction period and the beginning of the modern era, the easy-going ability, the humorous aggressiveness, the affable shrewdness of the two brothers provided an interlude of reconciliation that was healthful for the whole state. The pleasure of the public was voiced in the statement of a rural editor who asked, "Why not have a little fun as we go along?" and the public's gratitude

was shown in the subsequent careers of the two men. Bob won the 1886 race; he later served two more terms as governor, and single terms as congressman and senator, while Alf went on to serve once as governor and three times as congressman.

It was the brothers' showmanship—another asset highly prized in the politics of the Border States—that captivated their audiences and lingered in the memory and conversation of all who saw them. The fact that Bob was somewhat the better at "unpruned rhetoric," fiddle-playing and practical joking probably explains his victory in 1886, but one Memphis editor may have summed up the reason for Bob's enduring popularity when he said, "Our Bob tells the truth but knows how to make it palatable."

Actually, Bob Taylor had already displayed that talent before the campaign. Appointed United States pension agent at Knoxville just prior to the War of the Roses, Bob had anxiously awaited the advent of the needed income, but the appointment was slow in being processed. After a long wait he sent a one-line telegram to President Grover Cleveland: "That other fellow is still drawing my pay." (The appointment came the next day.) Later, when the Democratic committee wired to ask Bob if he would accept the nomination for governor, he replied, "A seedy individual whom we once knew appeared at my mother's home and said, 'Emerline, effen you don't believe I can carry a ham home, just try me.'"

In the campaign itself, Bob's orations included a speech which became a classic of Southern rhetoric: "The Fiddle and the Bow." Reveling in pathos and purple passages and accompanied by his own fiddling virtuosity, he drew verbal pictures of America's concert halls and mountain schools, Maine's dark pines and the Southland where "magnolia breezes blow," and all the wonders stretched across this great country—then salted the whole with laughter by quoting a lanky mountain man who shouted in the audience one night, "Let 'er stretch, durn 'er, hurrah for the Dimocratick party!"

Stealing each other's speeches, outwitting each other at country taverns and hospitable farmhouses, relieving the hardship and isolation of many a back-country Tennessean, Bob and Alf Taylor set a distinctive style of regional politicking. They capitalized on their humor, which always won special attention in Border States politics. Humor has always been the savor by which life in the more sophisticated areas was given spe-

Campaigning for the Senate in 1948, Estes Kefauver of Tennessee inveighs against boss E. H. Crump. Compared by Crump to a "pet coon," Kefauver donned a coonskin cap and went on to win the election.

cial style and zest; it has been the release that brought color and relaxation to harsher lives.

Humor has also been a by-product of the personal quality of politics in the Border States. Voters there have wanted to see their candidates at close range. Thus, early in the political career that carried him to the Presidency, James Monroe was advised by a knowledgeable uncle that "it would be indispensably necessary you should be in the County before the election and attend it when made."

Generations later, Estes Kefauver could break the power of the Crump machine in Tennessee and become a United States senator because—among other things—he capitalized on the personal predilections of the region. Likened by boss Crump to a "pet coon" that "puts its foot in an open drawer in your room, but invariably turns its head while its foot is feeling around in the drawer," Kefauver retorted that at least he was not Crump's pet coon. During the remainder of the campaign, in the words of political scientist V.O. Key, "Kefauver put on a coonskin cap, honorable badge of the pioneer, and made political hay." His seemingly boundless energy in shaking hands and his ability to convince people that he was genuinely concerned with their problems be-

came legendary. Kefauver's style was ridiculed in some Eastern and urban circles, but it kept him in the Senate until his death. And it enabled him to elevate his sights to such national campaigns as crusading against organized crime and monopolistic practices in the drug and power industries, and running as the Vice Presidential candidate in Adlai Stevenson's 1956 race for the Presidency.

The people of the Border States have, in fact, demonstrated a fondness for the bristling individualist in politics. The contradictions, inconsistencies and nonconformities that keep life flavorsome and interesting have enlivened the history of the region. It is noteworthy, for instance, that in the period prior to the Civil War, the most adamant states' righter and the strongest foe of the states-rights doctrine of nullification (the doctrine that a state had the right to declare federal legislation null and void) both came from the Border States. They were John Randolph of Virginia and Andrew Jackson of Tennessee. As befitted political leaders of the Border States, both men were rural in background, and both were fierce fighters. They had practically nothing else in common.

Tall, spare, arrogant John Randolph of Roanoke personified a strain in the Virginia tradition that displayed brilliance without warmth, eccentricity without creativeness, and power without humility. He was a master of the wit and invective that destroy—he had none of the humor that heals and redeems. Yet, in a time when oratory boasted Patrick Henry, Richard Henry Lee and John Marshall among its practicing performers, John Randolph was called the Orator of the Age.

Randolph summarized his personal and political philosophy in a sentence by which history has remembered him and all he represented: "I am an aristocrat; I love liberty, I hate equality." He felt that the separate states were the safest repositories of liberty and he held his allegiance to Virginia above all else. (When one of his plantation overseers used the abbreviation "Va." in addressing a letter, Randolph flew into a rage and tore the paper to bits. He wanted the name spelled out in proper dignity.)

"I [come] from a race who are known never to forsake a friend or forgive a foe," he said, and he proved himself a passionate hater. Of the Massachusetts Adamses, father and son, whom he assailed throughout their Presidencies, he vowed, "I bore some humble part in putting down the dynasty of John the First, and, by the Grace of God, I hope to aid in putting down the dynasty of John the Second." On another occasion, he described one of his many political opponents, Edward Livingston, then Secretary of State: "So brilliant, yet so corrupt, like rotten mackerel by moonlight, he shines and stinks."

As an inveterate nay-sayer, Randolph resisted, among other things, the War of 1812, the national bank, the Missouri Compromise, the tariff, all increases in the strength of the Army, and all internal improvements at federal expense. He never voted for admission of a single new state into the union. And he insisted, with characteristic acerbity, that "asking one of the states to surrender part of her sovereignty is like asking a lady to surrender part of her chastity."

Marshall Fishwick, keen and sympathetic observer of Virginians and their past, has placed Randolph in history for us: "Haughty John Randolph saw that the whole South, threatened by militant democracy and finance capitalism, was in what John C. Calhoun later called 'a period of transition.' . . . The Jeffersonian emphasis on equality and the natural goodness of man infuriated him. . . . Randolph fought change; Jefferson welcomed it. Randolph wanted to give the people order; Jefferson, light. It is hard to believe that the pessimism of Roanoke and the optimism of Monticello were products of the same society, indeed the same intermarried family—but they were."

Randolph grimly foresaw the rise of the democracy he despised. Until his death in 1833, he was steadfast in his belief that "Change is not reform," but four years earlier, in 1829, he had witnessed the greatest change in the Presidency since the birth of the United States. The first man of the west, the first representative of the self-made settlers of the frontier—Andrew Jackson—had taken over the reins of government. The colonial aristocracy (of Virginia gentry, New England theocrats, New York patroons and South Carolina Huguenots), the Federalist aristocracy (of George Washington, John Adams and Alexander Hamilton) and even the Jeffersonian enlightenment (of Jefferson, Madison and Monroe) had to give way as the common people invaded Washington and the White House at the inauguration ("Mud on the carpets!" cried shocked observers. "Broken furniture!"). Jackson had launched a new era in America, and the country would never be the same again.

It is a tribute to both men that President Jackson (out of the west that John Randolph abhorred) appointed the Virginian (whose politics he despised) to be American minister to Russia in

A staunch states' righter, U.S. Senator Harry Flood Byrd addresses his orchard workers at a picnic in 1958. Until his retirement in 1965, Byrd led the powerful Democratic machine that has dominated Virginia politics for most of this century.

1830. Randolph accepted graciously. The official friendship was short-lived, however. Taken ill soon after starting his tour of duty in St. Petersburg, Randolph came back to the U.S. and resigned, and shortly thereafter he attacked the President for the latter's stand against nullification. Randolph's shrewd and bitter vision caught the essential issue of his century. "I look for civil war," he wrote, the year before he died.

But "Old Hickory" would not permit civil war during his administrations. By threat, by reason and by the power of his own personality, he held the United States together—the wilderness west he knew in his blood, the financial East he distrusted by instinct, the plantation South he would not palliate and the industrial North he would not court. He was an authentic voice of the Border States. In him blazed all the hair-trigger temper, pride and rural individualism of the region.

Jackson was the first President whose family name meant only what he himself could make it mean. At the age of 15, the gangling, sandy-haired boy was an orphan who had already suffered imprisonment by the British, the horrors of smallpox and the slash of a sword from a British officer when he had refused to polish the redcoat's boots. He studied law in Salisbury, North Carolina, and in

1788, at the age of 21, he moved to the burgeoning area that would become Tennessee. He had found his home. Eventually he would build the Hermitage, an impressive but not ostentatious mansion, amid the rolling meadows near Nashville. It would, he thought, be a sanctuary for himself and his beloved wife, Rachel, who had come to middle Tennessee on the famous flatboat *Adventure*, commanded by her father, John Donelson.

As victor of the Battle of New Orleans in the War of 1812, Old Hickory won the wild acclaim of the Border States—and the U.S. His passionate constancy as enemy or friend endeared him to the voters of the Backwater. They admired a man who could "talk like a pirate and act like a Presbyterian." In a duel, Jackson killed a man who questioned his honor. In government he had a natural understanding of the people. "They were his blood relations," said his Presidential successor, Martin Van Buren, and added, "the only blood relations he had."

After tests on the battlefield, struggles in the courtrooms and service in the House and Senate, Jackson was elected to the Presidency in 1828. Rachel had died shortly before the inauguration and it was a lonely, sick man, fortified only by courage and convictions, who assumed the leadership of the country. He confronted crises without flinching and he grew in greatness to match the challenges and responsibilities of his office.

Issues of basic importance demanded resolution: the tariff, internal improvements, the disposal of western lands, the national bank and nullification. The last two questions—the Second Bank of the United States, which held well-nigh dictatorial control over the national economy, and the doctrine of nullification, espoused by South Carolina's John C. Calhoun—stirred the sharpest struggles and led to Jackson's most resounding victories. When he proved that the power of the United States government would prevail over the power centralized in the bank, Jackson won the devotion of western farmers and Eastern workingmen. When, in 1832, he met South Carolina's threat to nullify the tariff laws by sending eight ships to Charleston harbor and threatening to dispatch troops into South Carolina, he backed up the pledge he had made two years earlier: "Our Federal Union—it must and shall be preserved."

Jackson departed Washington in 1837 with the power of the bank destroyed and nullification nullified. The federal government was out of debt, its taxes were low and it had the confidence of the common man. Jackson arrived back at the Hermitage with $90 in cash and two pathetic mementos of his life with Rachel—her miniature portrait and her Bible. His cotton crop had been sold to pay debts in Washington. But he carried with him only one regret: that he had not been able to shoot Henry Clay or hang John C. Calhoun.

Two visitors—a tall Texan and a little boy—arrived at the Hermitage just after Jackson's death on an early summer day in 1845. Sam Houston, the greatest of the old general's frontier captains, had made a hard journey from Texas with his son in a vain attempt to pay his respects at the Hermitage while Old Hickory still lived. He was not ashamed to shed tears when he saw Jackson's bony form stretched on its deathbed. He drew his son up beside him and said, "Try to remember that you have looked on the face of Andrew Jackson."

Neither the Border States, nor all America, would forget Old Hickory easily: the tall, thin figure that, on foot or horseback, commanded an easy, natural authority; the crest of white hair swept straight back from his forehead, accentuating the long blade of his face and sharp blue eyes. They would not forget the towering tempers, which, in later years, were often manufactured as diversions to avoid futile argument, or the romantic devotion he had paid throughout his lifetime to his gentle Rachel. One of his biographers wrote that 15 years after Jackson's death people in the backwoods still came to the polls each election day and happily cast their votes for Andy Jackson.

A century later another President looked back upon the rise of Jacksonian democracy and spoke of the seventh President's "amazing personality." Franklin D. Roosevelt declared that the country's greatest legacy from Andrew Jackson was "his unending contribution to the vitality of our democracy." Vitality—it is the key word, perhaps, to describe the varied, paradoxical, vivid and intense politics of the Border States. The region has had its latter-day bosses and machines—paternalistic Ed Crump in Tennessee; frugal, autocratic Harry Byrd in Virginia; numerous county fiefdoms in Kentucky—but it has not nurtured the uglier demagogues who have tainted politics elsewhere in America. Instead, the region produced the Renaissance versatility of Thomas Jefferson, the aristocratic arrogance of John Randolph, the democratic dynamism of Andrew Jackson, the scholarly idealism of Woodrow Wilson. At times it has achieved greatness. And, more often than not, it has managed to "have a little fun" as it went along.

THE WELLSPRING OF A NATION

During the precarious years when the United States won its freedom and organized its government, it turned again and again for leadership to Virginia. There it found many of the extraordinary men the times demanded: a gifted executive to lead an army and a government; a pragmatist to place practicality above passion; a lawgiver to translate ideals into reality; two dissenters to point out shortcomings; an intellectual to provide perspective and scope. This remarkable band of Virginians, memorialized in the busts below, all lived within 200 miles of one another.

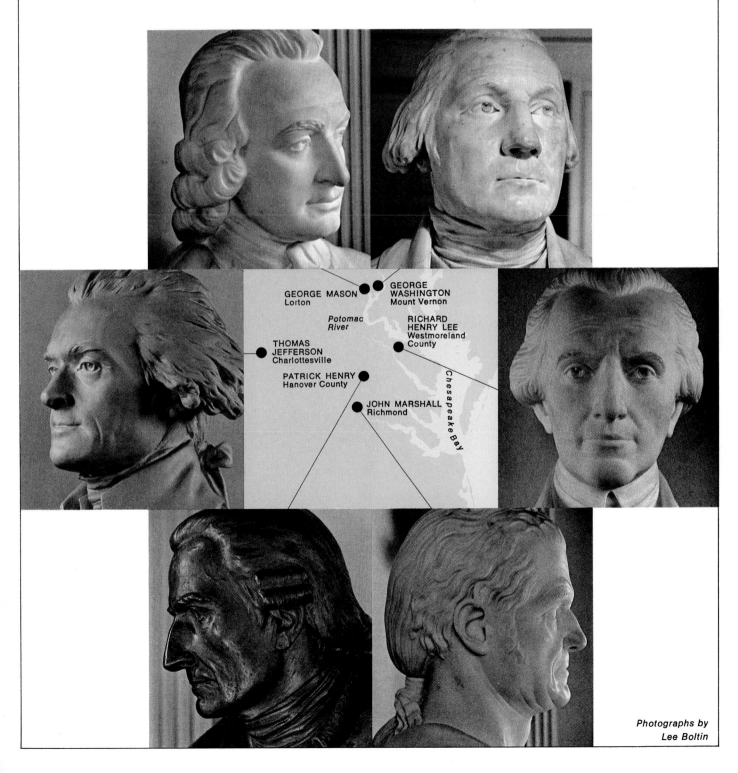

GEORGE MASON
Lorton

GEORGE WASHINGTON
Mount Vernon

Potomac River

RICHARD HENRY LEE
Westmoreland County

THOMAS JEFFERSON
Charlottesville

PATRICK HENRY
Hanover County

JOHN MARSHALL
Richmond

Chesapeake Bay

*Photographs by
Lee Boltin*

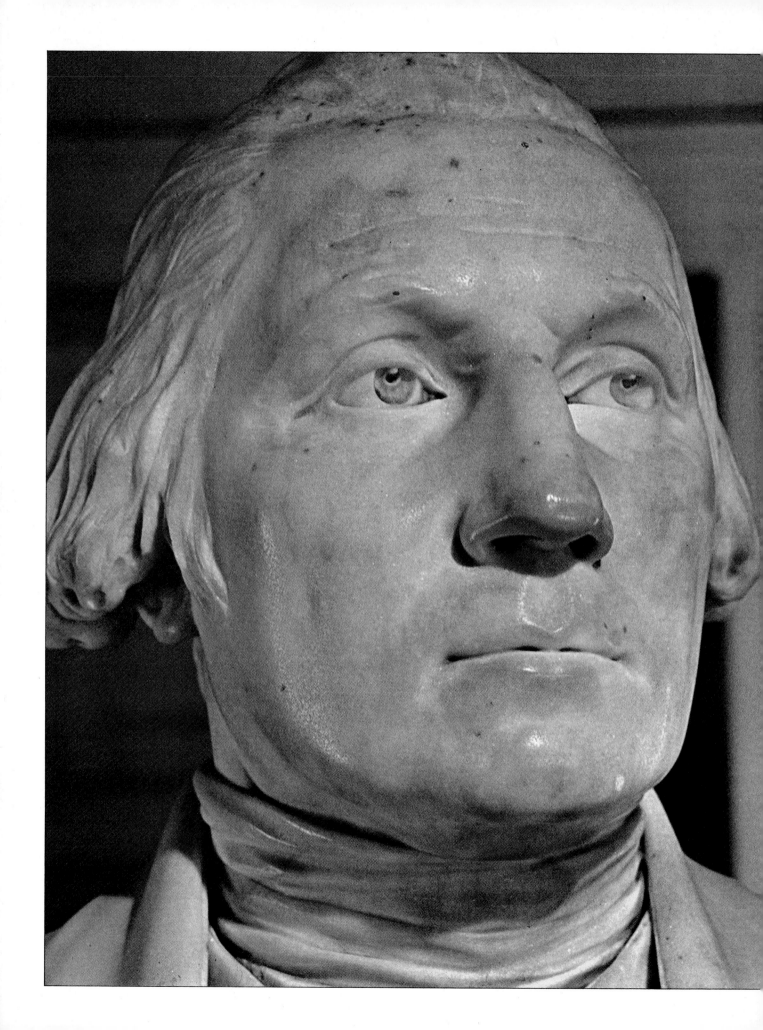

THE EXECUTIVE: GEORGE WASHINGTON

Heavy Cannon, Ordnance Stores and Ammunition to a pretty large Amount, are now forwarding. . . . In Order to introduce some kind of System and Method in our Supplies . . . I shall send forward the Heads of Departments as soon as their presence can be dispensed with. . . . In my progress to the Southward, I shall . . . make all the Arrangements necessary for the Operation in view [the siege of Yorktown]. . . . Should the retreat of Lord Cornwallis by water be cut off by the arrival of either of the French Fleets, I am persuaded you will do all in your power to prevent his escape by land.

Letter to Lafayette, September 2, 1781

In the appointments to the great offices of the government, my aim has been to combine geographical situations, and sometimes other considerations, with abilities and fitness of known characters.

Letter to Edward Carrington, October 9, 1795

In 1775, struggling for life, the amorphous, battle-born nation needed a commander who could forge an effective army from a raw rabble of poorly trained militia. In 1787, its freedom won, it needed a skilled mediator to preside over the formation of a new system of government. And in 1788, its daring Constitution ratified, it needed a strong President to prove at home and abroad that the system would work. It got all three in the person of George Washington of Virginia.

In each case Washington could say, as he said when assuming command of the Continental Army, that he was undertaking a task "too boundless for my abilities and far, very far beyond my experience." He approached his tasks with the reluctance of an aristocrat who longed for the life of a gentleman-farmer on his Mount Vernon estate, but he brought to these tasks the dedication and skills of a man bred to leadership. Methodical rather than inspired, efficient rather than brilliant, Washington found and applied workable, often ingenious, solutions to the problems that constantly confronted him.

One such Washingtonian solution resulted in the final victory of the Revolution. In 1781 Washington had his army poised to recapture New York City, but the French fleet that was to provide support for his attack turned up at the mouth of Chesapeake Bay, 340 miles to the south. Immediately, Washington changed his plans. He personally supervised the movement of his army to Yorktown *(see letter to Lafayette, above),* and his unexpected appearance there—along with that of the errant fleet—forced Lord Cornwallis to surrender his besieged army. The triumph virtually ended the war.

Shortly after the war, Washington's executive skills proved equally valuable in another context. As president of the Constitutional Convention of 1787, he moderated the discussions of fiercely opposed advocates of strong and weak federal government and helped to produce the compromise that remains the basic law of the United States.

Washington's last, perhaps greatest, legacy was his concept and conduct of the role of the President. The office is loosely defined in the Constitution, but it was Washington who made it that of the nation's chief executive, rather than that of a ceremonial figurehead. He gave a new nation leadership and direction, and established a model of power, style and responsibility that has been followed by his successors to this day.

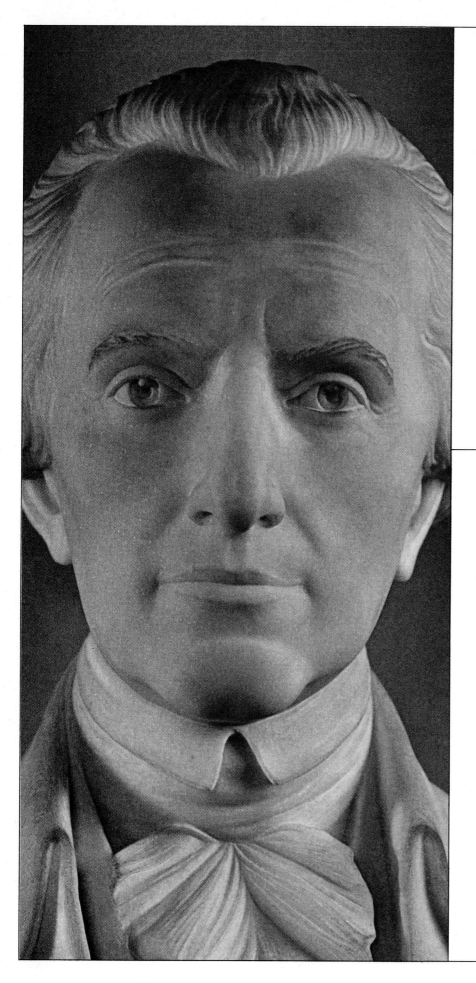

THE PRAGMATIST: RICHARD HENRY LEE

"The hasty, unpersevering, aristocratic genius of the south suits not my disposition," wrote Richard Henry Lee, member of one of Virginia's wealthiest and most distinguished families. Lee's own "disposition" incorporated a vein of pragmatism more in keeping with New England than with Tidewater Virginia. A radical but not a firebrand, a philosopher but not a visionary, Lee was able to link such dynamic but diverse men as Patrick Henry, Thomas Jefferson and Samuel Adams in the cause of American independence. It was typical of Lee's pragmatism that, after preparing the historic resolution *(below)* calling for independence, he left the writing of the Declaration itself to Jefferson and returned to Virginia to help assemble the new state government. The ancestral home at Stratford, where Lee was born, would later also be the birthplace of his celebrated kinsman Robert E. Lee.

Resolved

That these United Colonies are, and of right ought to be, free and independent States, that they are absolved from all allegiance to the British Crown, and that all political connection between them and the State of Great Britain is, and ought to be, totally dissolved.

That it is expedient forthwith to take the most effectual measures for forming foreign Alliances.

That a plan of confederation be prepared and transmitted to the respective Colonies for their consideration and approbation.

Resolution to Continental Congress, June 7, 1776

THE LAWGIVER: JOHN MARSHALL

In the early years of the 19th Century, the Constitution was virtually repudiated as the fundamental law of the land by a powerful states' rights movement that swept the nation. The fact that it not only survived, but emerged as an even stronger and more significant document than its creators had intended, is a monument to the persistence and vision of a single man, John Marshall.

As Chief Justice of the Supreme Court from 1801 to 1835, the self-taught Richmond lawyer put muscle and soul into the document he was called upon to interpret. In a series of landmark decisions, Marshall decreed that the Constitution was the country's supreme law, that all other laws must conform to it, and that its meaning was, in effect, whatever the Supreme Court said it was. In his hands, the Constitution became a code of living law, adaptable to the ever-changing needs of the nation.

All those who have framed written constitutions contemplate them as forming the fundamental and paramount law of the nation, and consequently the theory of every such government must be that an act of the legislature, repugnant to the constitution, is void.

Marbury v. Madison, 1801

That this court does not usurp power is most true. That this court dares not shrink from its duty is not less true.

Aaron Burr trial, 1807

The Constitution and laws of a State, so far as they are repugnant to the Constitution and laws of the United States, are absolutely void.

Cohens v. Virginia, 1821

THE DISSENTERS: PATRICK HENRY AND GEORGE MASON

While patriotic voices of unity were responsible for the creation of the Constitution, equally patriotic voices of dissent were quick to see its flaws and to urge needed changes that eventually took the form of the Bill of Rights. The most articulate of these dissenters was Patrick Henry. The same golden voice that in 1775 uttered ''Give me liberty or give me death!'' spoke the equally impassioned words quoted below during an unsuccessful fight to block Virginia's ratification of the Constitution 13 years later.

The ratification fight was the last stormy chapter in a lifetime of dissent—dissent against tax-supported clergy, against greedy Tidewater landowners, against oppressive British rule. Over the years, Henry's dissenting voice brought him from a frontier law practice to the heights of power and prestige—and then returned him to comparative oblivion. A maverick to the end, he later became a Federalist and delivered his last speeches in defense of the Constitution he once had scorned.

Old as I am . . . I may yet have the appellation of "rebel". . . . As this government [the Constitution] stands, I despise and abhor it.

The question turns on that poor little thing—the expression We, the "people" instead of the "states."

I see the awful immensity . . . with which it [the Constitution] is pregnant. I see it. I feel it. I see beings of a higher order anxious concerning our decision.

If I shall be in the minority, I shall have those painful sensations which arise from . . . being overpowered in a good cause.

Speeches at the Virginia Ratification Convention, 1788

The name of George Mason does not appear among the signers of the Constitution. Its omission reflects an act of courageous dissent rarely equalled in American history. The revered elder statesman of Virginia, Mason had been one of the moving forces at the Constitutional Convention. Yet he refused to endorse the document produced there, because it lacked specific guarantees of human rights.

Mason's opposition split the ranks of Virginia aristocracy and temporarily cost him the friendship of his neighbor George Washington. Undaunted, he carried his crusade to the Virginia ratification convention where he argued the need for basic amendments to the Constitution, earning Thomas Jefferson's praise as "of the first order of greatness." Exhausted and gout-ridden, Mason then retired to his Gunston Hall estate. He lived just long enough to see the Bill of Rights —drawn largely from the Virginia Declaration of Rights he had written in 1776—incorporated into the law of the land.

All men are created equally free and independent, and have certain inherent rights, of which they cannot, by any compact, deprive or divest their posterity; among which are the enjoyment of life and liberty, with the means of acquiring and possessing property, and pursuing and obtaining happiness and safety.

Original draft, Virginia Declaration of Rights, 1776

I would have lost this hand before it should have marked my name to the new government.

Quoted in the *Pennsylvania Packet,* November 10, 1787

I would not forfeit the approbation of my own mind for the approbation of any man, or all the men upon earth.

Letter to his son John, March 13, 1789

TH INT LL CTUAL: THOMAS J SON

I have sworn upon the altar of God, eternal hostility against every form of tyranny over the mind of man.

Letter to Dr. Benjamin Rush, September 23, 1800

Nothing would do more extensive good at small expense than the establishment of a small, circulating library in every county, to consist of a few, well-chosen books to be lent . . . under such regulations as would secure their safe return in due time.

Letter to John Wythe, May 19, 1809

Nature intended me for the tranquil pursuits of science by rendering them my supreme delight.

Letter to Pierre DuPont de Nemours, March 2, 1809

Knowledge is power . . . knowledge is safety, and . . . knowledge is happiness.

Letter to George Ticknor, November 25, 1817

In any age Thomas Jefferson would have been a remarkable man; in the America of the late 18th and early 19th Centuries, he was a titan. Master of six languages, owner of 8,000 books, scholar of the classics, scientist, inventor, philosopher, musician, architect, gardener and art patron, Jefferson towered over even the best-educated Virginia aristocrats.

This inveterate intellectual, devoted to "the tranquil pursuits of science," played an important public role in American history as President and as the founder of what is now the Democratic Party—yet he had a lifelong dislike for public life. Shy, humorless, a poor speaker, he seemed miscast among the gifted leaders and orators of his day.

But Jefferson made contributions to his nation that only an intellectual could make. Few other men could have written a statement of national purpose as clear, concise and eloquent as the Declaration of Independence. Using "neither book nor pamphlet," but incorporating earlier statements by fellow-Virginians George Mason and Richard Henry

Lee, he drew up the document that has become the cornerstone of the country's political heritage.

From the 17th Century philosopher John Locke, Jefferson inherited a strong belief in the perfectability of man—the idea that, given knowledge, men could govern themselves. To provide that knowledge, Jefferson advocated systems of public schools and libraries that were regarded as visionary in his time. He himself regarded his role as founder of the University of Virginia—whose buildings he designed—as an accomplishment on a par with his authorship of the Declaration.

When Jefferson completed his second Presidential term in 1809, he fled from public life to his beloved books at Monticello like a "prisoner released from his chains." Nevertheless, a grateful nation and an amazing stroke of fate have combined to link him forever with the birth of the United States. Thomas Jefferson's death was to come on July 4, 1826—exactly 50 years from the day the Declaration of Independence was signed.

4

The Cruel Division

The land scarred by civil war is healed now. The water of Bloody Pond at Shiloh stands clear and quiet; beneath the tender green shade of the Wilderness, fragile pink lady's-slippers and purple violets bloom each spring. Dogwood laces the woods fringing Manassas and Missionary Ridge; and from Fort Henry on the Tennessee River and Fort Donelson on the Cumberland to Fort Fisher on the Atlantic Coast, grass cushions the mounds and hollows of old trenches.

But in the American convulsion known as the Civil War, the Border States lay at the heart of the agony. More battles were fought in Virginia and Tennessee than in all the other states put together, more Confederate deaths were suffered by North Carolina than by any other state, Kentucky was one of the strategic areas vital to the war, and West Virginia was born in an internal conflict that tore away a third of the Old Dominion. The Presidents of both the United and Confederate States were born in Kentucky, scarcely a hundred miles and a single year apart. The Border States pro-

vided most of the military heroes who, in certain quarters, have made the Civil War more potent as myth than as history.

The cruel division among the American people, reflected most specifically among the people of the Border States, did not begin with the shot fired at Fort Sumter in April 1861, nor did it end with the simple exchange at Appomattox Courthouse four Aprils later. The internal division dated from the beginning of the American colonies, grew through successive stages of increasing intensity until its angry culmination in the Civil War, and continues today in struggles over civil rights and equal opportunity.

First, there was the division of black from white: a fundamental schism established and maintained by the slave system and its implicit assertion that to be black was to be less than human.

Second, there was the division of Southern white from Southern white: a difference which revealed not only a North-South conflict but also a confrontation between East and West. And the sharpest cutting edge of this separation was to be found in the Border States.

Third, there was the ultimate division of war itself: a strange compound of the accidental and the inevitable, horror and heroism, futility and

At Knoxville, in 1861, simultaneous recruiting of soldiers for the Union *(foreground)* and the Confederacy *(background)* reveals the divided loyalties of east Tennessee on the eve of the Civil War. This sketch was drawn by an eyewitness.

triumph, finally interwoven into a pattern called history.

When the Civil War limped to a close, two questions about America were settled: there would be no slavery, there would be a single country—North and South, East and West. But other questions then arose—questions of Negro rights and opportunities. These questions remain unresolved more than a century later and the Border States are playing a crucial role in their final settlement.

There can be no understanding of the Border States without an insight into the divisions its people helped to create, and with which they have grappled in agony and blood.

At the root of all these divisions was the one between Negro and white.

If, as historian Charles G. Sellers Jr. has said, "The key to the tragedy of southern history is the paradox of the slaveholding South's devotion to 'liberty,'" then that tragedy was most fully enacted in the Border State of Virginia. By the 1790s Virginia had 270,000 slaves and 296,000 free citizens—and it was entering a period of severe depression. The middle of the 18th Century had been the golden period of the state's tobacco aristocracy, but tobacco is a hungry plant, rapidly consuming the fertility of the soil. And as quick riches whetted the appetites of the planters for more luxuries, so the demands of tobacco necessitated the clearing of more acres of new ground. Exhausted land and extravagant tastes combined to create a precarious existence. In the years after the Revolution, Virginia found thousands of its vast acres worn out and abandoned. John Randolph wrote that the plantations he loved so well had become "one desolate expanse of dismantled houses, abandoned fields, and mournful evergreens," and observed there were more deer and wild turkey in the country around Williamsburg than in Kentucky. In addition to the problem of its depleted land, Virginia encountered a glutted tobacco market abroad. With its heavy investments in slaves, and an almost equal number of blacks and whites within its borders, the state faced the possible collapse of its economy.

Then three events took place in close succession. In 1790 the importation of a silky "long-staple" strain of cotton, which grew well in such states as Georgia and South Carolina, opened parts of the Southeast to cotton production. In 1793 a young Yankee schoolteacher named Eli Whitney invented the cotton gin, which separated cotton fibers from seed quickly and inexpensively and turned cotton into an enormously profitable crop. And in 1803 the United States negotiated the Louisiana Purchase, which added vast new lands to the cotton kingdom. The great single crop of the South was no longer tobacco, but cotton.

One response of many hard-pressed Virginians was to move to the new cotton plantations in large numbers. By 1832 the Lynchburg *Virginian* could report that "the constant emigration to the great West of our most substantial citizens, the bone and sinew of the country . . . is the daily subject of complaint among our mercantile men and of which our naked streets and untenanted houses are such emphatic evidence." But emigration was not Virginia's decisive response to the new developments. More important was its emergence as a slave-breeding state.

In 1808 the importation of slaves into America was outlawed. In the Deep South, cotton planters turned to the older slave states, and especially Virginia, for supplies of slave labor. By 1815 this domestic traffic played a major part in Virginia's economy; Negroes reared and trained there were highly prized. From its enlightened days of Revolutionary leadership, Virginia had traveled a long downhill road. In 1778 it had become the first community in the civilized modern world to outlaw traffic in slaves. But now Virginians were displaying an interest in the profitable slave traffic that made them perilously akin to the crass west they so often deplored. Indeed, Virginia was supplying that frontier with many of its slaves.

Many Virginians feared the outcome of this development. In their own consciences and on their daily ledgers, they faced the struggle between humanity and profit at close range. Thomas Jefferson said, "Indeed I tremble for my country when I reflect that God is just: that his justice cannot sleep forever." But he kept his slaves.

George Mason, the champion of the Bill of Rights, penetrated to the heart of the matter: "As nations can not be rewarded or punished in the next world they must be in this. By an inevitable chain of causes and effects providence punishes national sins, by national calamities." But he too kept his slaves.

In 1831-1832 the General Assembly of Virginia debated the question of slavery. Historian Avery Craven has said that during the debate, "men questioned the justice of slavery, blamed it for the weakened condition of agriculture, and declared that it drove lesser white men from the community, made labor a disgrace, and prevented the rise of a diversified economic life. . . . In the next three decades the most rabid New England reformers would be able to add little to [the exchange]." But words took the place of action. By a vote of 65 to 58 the question was finally tabled—and the members of the Assembly kept their slaves.

Aside from its futility, the Virginia Assembly debate illustrates the second large division festering within all the Border States: the sharp separation between white and white.

At first the division was focused chiefly upon the slavery question. Congregations of Methodists and Baptists opposed the concept of human bondage, but the chief protesters were the Quakers. Living largely in inland areas, the Quakers formed groups for the manumission, or emancipation, of the slaves and published antislavery newspapers. In 1815 they organized the Manumission Society of Tennessee and in 1816, the North Carolina Manumission Society, which soon boasted 28 branches. By 1827, in fact, there were more antislavery societies in North Carolina and Tennessee than in any other states in the Union.

Within a decade, however, antislavery protest in the Border States was diminishing. The North Carolina Manumission Society held its last meeting in 1834 and by 1837 there was not an antislavery society left in all the South. The power of the planter society—the society of the Virginia Tidewater, of eastern North Carolina, of Bluegrass Kentucky and Tennessee—had reasserted itself. Stirred by their fear of slave rebellion, stiffened in their angry pride by increasing attacks from Northern abolitionists, the planters successfully took the region out of the antislavery camp.

But the conflict between the large-scale planter and the small backwoods farmer was far from over. In the end, it was this conflict that caused the most acrimonious differences among the whites in the years leading up to the Civil War. The differences demonstrated that the tensions troubling the country were not only between North and South but also, and in some areas even more critically, between East and West.

Despite the popular image to the contrary, the sprawling, luxurious, affluent plantation was a rarity rather than a commonplace, not only in the Border States but throughout the South. In 1860 there were fewer than 385,000 owners of slaves in the entire South—one quarter of the white population. Among these slaveowners, 88 per cent held fewer than 20 slaves each. Three fourths of the South's white population were yeoman farmers, many of them living in the western parts of the Border States. For these farmers, slavery itself was not an urgent issue. When they opposed slavery—and some of them did—their opposition was more a matter of economics than of morality. What was more important, their conflict with the planting oligarchy often led them to look to the national rather than to the state government for direction and aid. Whether they were proslavery or antislavery, the western farmers were passionately pro-Union. And speaking for them, or from their point of view, were the most picturesque of the Southern dissenters.

One of these dissenters was a Louisville editor, George D. Prentice, who came to Kentucky from Connecticut to write a biography of Henry Clay, and stayed on to edit a new newspaper, the Louisville *Journal*. From the birth of his paper in 1830, Prentice fervently supported both slavery and the Union, apparently never perceiving that dissension over the one could threaten destruction of the other. One of his successors said that Prentice "was as ready to fight as to write, and his lot was cast where he had to do a great deal of both." During one month he fought three duels on the streets of Louisville. When the editor of a pro-secession paper fired at him one day without warning, Prentice shot the gun out of his assailant's hand, then coolly walked away, observing, "I will not harm an unarmed man."

In North Carolina the prevailing attitude was less open to dissent. When a soft-spoken chemistry professor, B. S. Hedrick of the University of North Carolina, let it be known in 1856 that he would vote for John C. Frémont, a Unionist "Black Republican," for President, he was burned in effigy by the students, fired by the trustees and almost tarred and feathered by his fellow townsmen.

Another North Carolinian may have welcomed the violent opposition he aroused. In 1857 Hinton Rowan Helper, born into the small-farmer class of North Carolina's Piedmont, published *The Impending Crisis of the South: How to Meet It*. Helper opposed slavery, not because he cared for the Negro but because he was concerned for impoverished white farmers. He vividly described the vicious circle produced by slavery: "It makes us poor; poverty makes us ignorant; ignorance makes us wretched; wretchedness makes us wicked, and wickedness leads us to the devil."

It was in Tennessee that the Southern voice for the Union became shrillest. Its leading trumpeter was a circuit-riding preacher, partisan editor, and fighting politician, William G. Brownlow, who described himself, just before the war, as being 55 years old but added: "I walk erect, have but few gray hairs, and look to be younger than any whiskey-drinking, tobacco-chewing, profane-swearing Secessionist in any of the Cotton States, of forty years." As a Methodist circuit rider in the Southern highlands, "Parson" Brownlow had engaged the enemy as he defined them: Baptists, Presbyterians, the devil and the Democrats. After founding a newspaper—the *Whig*—first in the village of Elizabethton in northeastern Tennessee, then in nearby Jonesboro and finally in the city of Knoxville, he added Northern abolitionists and Southern secessionists to the list. His motto was, "Independent in all things—Neutral in nothing," and the *Whig* had one of the largest circulations of any Southern newspaper.

In the 1850s Brownlow was both promising that he would die to preserve slavery and "exposing" Northerners as nonslaveholders because "their virtuous and pious minds were chiefly exercised in slave-stealing and slave-selling." By 1861, however, he was thundering: "I would as soon be engaged in importing the plague from the East, as in helping to build up a Southern Confederacy upon the ruins of the American Constitution." He warned that "the man who calculates upon peaceable dissolutions of the Union is either a madman or a fool," and he prophesied "the most fearful war that ever raged in the civilized world."

When Tennessee seceded from the Union, Brownlow began a scorching attack upon the Confederacy. He despised those who joined the state majority, and dared his opposition to carry out their threats: "If these God-forsaken scoundrels and hell-deserving assassins want satisfaction out of me for what I have said about them—and that has been no little—they can find me on these streets every day of my life but Sunday."

Only a deeply divided society could have tolerated such an editor in its midst. Brownlow was a true product of the Border States and of the schism between white and white that cut across the entire region. He personified the resentment of the western upland areas against the eastern lowland powers. Most of the upcountry men did not much want to fight either for Deep South planters or for Northeastern industrialists. But the war swept all into its holocaust. The culmination of the cruel divisions within the Border States came in the trial by fire by civil war.

After the attack on Fort Sumter, in the spring of 1861, the Border States had to decide whether to remain in the Union or join the Confederacy. The map at right, based on votes in state legislatures and conventions, shows that sympathies in the region were divided. Virginia was the first to act, voting for secession on April 17, but the northwest part of the state was so alienated by the move that it declared its independence on June 17th and eventually joined the Union as West Virginia. Kentucky voted to remain neutral, but in September Confederate troops violated its neutrality and the state swung to the Union. Although Tennessee's eastern counties were strongly sympathetic to the Union, it joined the Confederacy in May. North Carolina, surrounded by Confederate states, had no choice but to vote for secession.

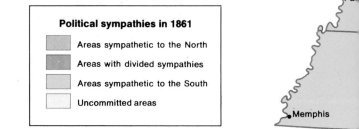

Political sympathies in 1861

Areas sympathetic to the North

Areas with divided sympathies

Areas sympathetic to the South

Uncommitted areas

Pa●

● Memphis

Distraught by internal divisions, the Border States reacted to the outbreak in disparate ways. Governor John Letcher of Virginia vowed that since Lincoln "had chosen to inaugurate civil war" he could have no troops from Virginia. Governor John W. Ellis of North Carolina replied that his state would not participate in this subjugation of the South and violation of the Constitution. There would be "no troops from North Carolina." Governor Isham G. Harris of Tennessee said, "Tennessee will not furnish a man for purposes of coercion, but 50,000, if necessary, for the defense of our rights, and those of our Southern brothers."

Despite staunch rhetoric, each of these states had a dissident minority of no small influence. Virginia's was concentrated chiefly in the west, and on June 17, 1861, in convention at Wheeling, that part of the state declared its independence. In 1863 Lincoln welcomed West Virginia into the Union as the 35th state.

North Carolina's reservations were less readily apparent. The state emerged from the Civil War with the claim that North Carolinians were "first at Bethel, farthest at Gettysburg and Chickamauga, and last at Appomattox." But its pride in its own independence made North Carolina a

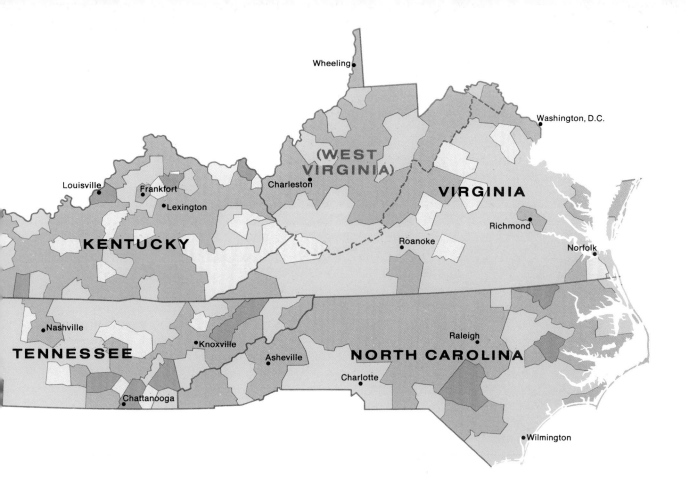

problem for the Richmond government throughout the war; its western areas were hotbeds of Union sentiment and many of its young men enlisted in the Federal Army.

In Tennessee when the popular vote on secession came in June, more than 100,000 voters favored joining the Confederacy. But more than 47,000 Tennesseans voted for the Union, and this minority was of no small consequence. Tennessee was the last state to leave the Union, and it was to furnish some 30,000 troops to the Union—more than Rhode Island, Delaware or Minnesota, and almost as many as New Hampshire or Vermont.

And what of Kentucky? This was truly a border state, bitterly divided between North and South and between East and West, with a Confederate governor and a pro-Union legislature. Its strategic importance was apparent to Lincoln, who was reported to have said that he hoped to have God on his side, but that he must have Kentucky. In September 1861, he learned that the state would fight for the Union side. A later military analyst, Edward Conrad Smith, has said that "South of the Ohio River there was no good line of defense for the Southern armies. From the time that Kentucky finally made her decision for the Union, they fought a losing battle."

So the Border States chose sides. Three of them joined the Confederacy; it was a confederacy that had nine million people (nearly 3.5 million of them Negro slaves) compared with 22 million in the Union; that had one third as much land as the Union, one fourth as much banking capital, less than half as many miles of railroad (and not a single "through railroad"), one half as much corn, one fourth as much wheat, and one tenth as much invested in factories; and that had not a single shipyard or munitions plant. The Rebel yell and "Dixie," together with the experience of Southern boys accustomed to an outdoor life and the knowledge that their homeland was being invaded: all these would create an asset called morale outweighing more tangible necessities—or so many Southerners believed in the first enthusiasm of war.

Paradoxically, Southern morale received its first blow from a victory. The first battle of Manassas (Bull Run) resulted in 4,600 casualties, a sobered North ("No more hurrahing, no more humbug," said a colonel named William Tecumseh Sherman, who had fought in the battle), and an exultant South. But the editor of the Richmond *Examiner* wrote in retrospect what Manassas had meant to the Confederacy: "The unfortunate victory was followed by a period of fancied security and of relaxed exertions. . . . Manassas proved the greatest misfortune that could have befallen the Confederacy."

Four long years stretched ahead, an orgy of death and destruction whose heaviest blows would fall on the Border States. In Virginia there were battles at places named Seven Pines (where Robert E. Lee took command of the Army of Northern Virginia), Malvern Hill (on whose slopes 5,500 Confederates fell under one day of Union artillery fire), Fredericksburg, Chancellorsville and the Wilderness, Spotsylvania (with its Bloody Angle), Yellow Tavern (where Jeb Stuart's Confederate plume fell to the dust), Cold Harbor (7,000 Union casualties in 30 minutes), Petersburg (the final Federal siege), and the surrender at Appomattox Courthouse. And in Virginia's rich Shenandoah Valley there were the legendary maneuvers of Stonewall Jackson's cavalry in 1862, when his 15,000 men kept some 50,000 Northern soldiers on the alert and ineffective. Later, Phil Sheridan's burn-and-destroy campaign reduced the fat barns of the Shenandoah to rubble and devastated the granary of the Confederacy.

But it was in the west that the outcome of the war was really decided—in Tennessee, particularly, where the early capture of Fort Henry on the Tennessee River and Fort Donelson on the Cumberland opened the Mississippi to Federal forces as far south as Memphis. In Tennessee there was Shiloh, a gory Confederate defeat more than a gory Union victory, the turning point for the South's hold in the west. There was Chattanooga, where Missionary Ridge, a fortified 300-foot escarpment, was overrun by 20,000 battle-scarred Northerners who disregarded both terrain and enemy fire and overlooked the fact that they had never received orders for their action. And there was Knoxville, where Federal troops rendered the rich valley of east Tennessee useless to the South, which desperately needed east Tennessee corn and bacon.

The war also proceeded on the home front. In the rough hill-country throughout the Border States the people were divided among themselves. Fathers and sons disowned each other, brothers fought in opposing armies, neighbor raided neighbor and bushwhackers and outlaws preyed on Union and Confederate families alike.

And in the three states which had joined the Confederacy, the old question still gnawed insistently: where did states' rights end and the central government's right become preeminent? It was one of the crucial questions upon which the Confederacy foundered. No single person was more identified with the problem than Zebulon B. Vance, the most popular state politician ever to hold office in North Carolina.

Vance was a mountain man, born in Buncombe County, in 1830. He was a big, barrel-chested, bull-necked man of style and zest, with an irrepressible sense of humor. As a young lawyer in Asheville, state legislator, Congressman, captain and colonel in the Confederate Army, and wartime governor, he used his earthy and pungent wit to carry him over many a hurdle and through numerous rough situations. The people of North Carolina relished his stories and his jokes, and they responded to his oratory. As governor, his complete dedication to the state and his courage in defending it from intruders—including both Northern soldiers and Confederate directives—won him the permanent devotion of his fellow Tar Heels.

Up to the firing on Fort Sumter, Vance opposed secession, but he refused to fight against his neighbors. He himself described his conversion, which took place in a small mountain town. "I was canvassing for the Union with all my strength; I was addressing a large and excited crowd, large numbers of whom were armed, and literally had my hand extended upward in pleading for peace and the Union of our Fathers, when the telegraphic news was announced of the firing on Sumter and the President's call for 75,000 volunteers. When my hand came down from that impassioned gesticulation, it fell slowly and sadly by the side of a Secessionist. I immediately, with altered voice and manner, called upon the assembled multitude to volunteer not to fight against but for South Carolina. I said, if war must come, I preferred to be with my own people."

There were times, however, when Jefferson Davis must have wondered whether, with friends like Vance, he needed enemies. North Carolina's chief executive quarreled with the Richmond government over the appointment of Virginia officers to command North Carolina troops, over the impressment of private property and, most important, over the Confederacy's conscription laws and its suspension of the writ of habeas corpus. He threatened to take North Carolina out of the Confederacy—a little secession rebellion within the larger secession rebellion. At one point Davis requested an end to all correspondence between himself and Vance. The relationship endured,

PAULINE CUSHMAN

BELLE BOYD

During the Civil War both the Union and the Confederacy employed alluring female spies. Two of the most remarkable operated in the Border States. Pauline Cushman, a celebrated actress before the war, frequented Army camps in Tennessee, attracting the attention of Southern officers and prying military secrets from them. In later life, wearing the uniform of a Union major, she lectured about her wartime experiences. Belle Boyd, an honorary captain of the Confederacy, crossed battle lines under fire to bring General "Stonewall" Jackson news of an impending attack near Front Royal, Virginia. After the war Belle, too, became a successful actress.

however, despite all its strains and Vance's state stayed with the Confederacy. Although it had only one ninth of the Confederacy's population, it suffered nearly a fourth of all the battle deaths.

For the mountain people who were Union sympathizers during the war, Vance sought toleration rather than retaliation. He inspired his people to hard work, and they fed and clothed themselves as well or better than any other Southern state. On the battlefield he aroused soldiers to heights of fervor. After one visit to Jeb Stuart's men in the field, that cavalry hero pronounced Vance the greatest orator who ever lived. And after the war and a period of imprisonment during the Reconstruction era, Vance continued fighting for his people as governor for a third term and as U.S. Senator through four terms.

After all, it was the individual's freedoms and his rights, protected so vigilantly by Zebulon Vance, that had been at the heart of the war. At the close of the war, however, ominous developments threatened these freedoms and rights in the Border States. In Pulaski, Tennessee, in the dark December of 1865, a group of bored young men gathered in a deserted house and formed a secret society to ride anonymously around the countryside. They devised outlandish titles and oaths and

initiation rituals. But what had begun as "entertainment" was soon transformed into a harsh system of extra-legal control. Its perpetrators called themselves the Ku Klux Klan. As they rode under their white sheets and tall peaked hoods, on horses with muffled hooves, they devised a potent weapon to rule a region where the majority of the people were rural and superstitious. The weapon was terror.

The weird visitations of the KKK and their use of violence were directed almost solely toward keeping Negroes, especially those intending to vote, in "their place." The organization spread rapidly to other parts of the South. In 1867 Nathan Bedford Forrest of Tennessee, who had been called the "Wizard of the Saddle" as a general in the Confederate Army, became Grand Wizard of the KKK. Within two years he found himself in such opposition to the Klan's methods that he resigned. Forrest called for other members to follow his example and dissolve the secret society, but his advice was not heeded. The KKK later dissolved and then reappeared, and its resurgence has marked every period of transition and tension that the region has undergone.

The end of Reconstruction in 1877 left a bitter division within the Border States. The Negro was legally emancipated, but he was still in bondage—to illiteracy, to a backward agriculture, to the breakdown of his family structure and to the poverty of a region raked by war. As historian John Hope Franklin has pointed out, "In failing to provide adequate economic security for the freedmen, Reconstruction left them no alternative but to submit to their old masters, a submission that made easier the efforts of Southern whites to overthrow Reconstruction and restore a system based on white supremacy."

Though the Civil War settled the questions of secession and chattel slavery, it did not settle the issue of the Negro's status in the South. That issue was resolved in a series of arrangements—many of them hardened into the formality of law—by which the old inferiorities of slavery were perpetuated in the injustices of segregation. These so-called Jim Crow laws made their first appearance in the Border States.

Jim Crow did not spring into being, fully realized and rigid, at the end of the war or even at the conclusion of the Reconstruction era. From the 1870s to the 1890s, Negroes were voting in large numbers, encouraged by white leaders of opposing parties who solicited their vote.

In 1885 a Negro newspaperman named T. McCants Stewart made a trip through Virginia and North Carolina. In both states he found himself treated as an equal by the whites. He reported to his New York paper that he had "put a chip on his shoulder," but neither the white Virginian who asked to sit beside him on the train nor the white diners with whom he ate in a station dining room near Petersburg, Virginia, disturbed that chip. Stewart's experiences in the Old Dominion and in neighboring North Carolina led him to believe that "the whites of the South are really less afraid to [have] contact with colored people than the whites of the North."

Similarly, in 1886, the Richmond *Dispatch* asserted that "nobody here objects to serving on juries with negroes," and said that Negroes sat in both branches of the legislature, "as they have a right to sit."

By 1900, however, the Richmond *Times* was calling for segregation "in every relation of Southern life," and argued that "God Almighty drew the color line and it cannot be obliterated." By that date the Negro was banned throughout the South from white hotels, restaurants, places of amusement, barber shops, theaters—and public schools. In 1896, by its "separate but equal" doc-trine in the case of *Plessy* v. *Ferguson,* the Supreme Court gave the nation's highest sanction to the principle of segregation.

What brought about this change in the customs and atmosphere of the Border States between the close of the war and the turn of the century? Historian C. Vann Woodward has summarized the influences succinctly in *The Strange Career of Jim Crow.* He said the "adoption of extreme racism was due not so much to a conversion as it was to a relaxation of the opposition. All the elements of fear, jealousy, proscription, hatred, and fanaticism had long been present, as they are present in various degrees of intensity in any society. What enabled them to rise to dominance was not so much cleverness or ingenuity as it was a general weakening and discrediting of the numerous forces that had hitherto kept them in check. The restraining forces included not only Northern liberal opinion in the press, the courts, and the government, but also internal checks imposed by the prestige and influence of the Southern conservatives, as well as by the idealism and zeal of the Southern radicals."

For all their evasions, neither the Border States nor the South as a whole could bring itself to proscribe education for Negroes. During the Reconstruction era, for example, Negro colleges were established in the region. One of the most successful, Fisk University in Nashville, Tennessee, became world famous for its Jubilee Singers, who presented concerts across the United States and in Europe. Ironically, however, in founding all-Negro colleges, philanthropists and the federal government were promoting segregation.

Negro public schools, to make matters worse, were not only segregated but impoverished. To some extent, their poverty arose from the fact that they were dependent upon one of the poorest regions of the United States. In any comparison with national standards, and especially with those of the Northeast, all the education of the Border States was inferior. At the turn of the century, the average yearly school attendance of a North Carolina child was about 22 days, only a fifth as long as that of a child in Massachusetts. Based on its school population, North Carolina spent $1.64 annually per child for education; Massachusetts spent $21.55 per child. The average daily expenditure per pupil in Virginia was 8.2 cents; in Massachusetts it was 20 cents. North Carolina valued its school property at $1.64 for each child, and Virginia at $5.33, while Massachusetts valued its school property at $60.92 per child.

But within the Border States, discrepancies between white and Negro education were equally glaring. In North Carolina white teachers received slightly less than $100 per year; Negro teachers received $64.42 a year. And if city schools were poor, backwoods country schools were bleak indeed, while Negro rural schools were sometimes incredibly inadequate. In 1915 in Amelia County, Virginia, for every dollar spent on teaching a Negro child, $12.37 was spent on a white child.

In 1902 a North Carolina newspaper foretold, perhaps more clearly than it realized, the shape of things to come. "Education," it said, "has but one tendency: to give higher hopes and aspirations. There can be but one result in educating the negro." Candidly admitting that higher aspirations were not the result that that paper and its white readers desired, the editorial stated, "We want the negro to remain here, just about as he is —with mighty little change. We want them to become better cooks, better servants, better wash women, better workmen in farm and field and shop. We will cheerfully pay taxes to give him that sort of schooling." And the paper added, with insight rare in the South, "But that is not what the negro wants."

Indeed it was not. Although he experienced another half-century or more of restricted voting, inadequate schools and health facilities, segregation in every area of public life and limited opportunities for employment and housing, this was "not what the negro" wanted. By 1930 the gap between white and Negro schools had reached its widest gulf. During the Great Depression, wrenching disparities had appeared in all the economy and society, but again, the hardships had fallen most calamitously on the Negro. In 1935 approximately a quarter of the million and a half Negro domestic workers were on relief; in one corner of the Border States, in Norfolk, Virginia, 80 per cent of all employable Negroes were on relief.

This plight was relieved in part by the economic resurgence brought by World War II—but the war also stimulated the rising demands of American Negroes and the country could not answer them. In 1945 the Border States and the South emerged from the war, as one resident said, "with more social change and more unfinished business than any other part of the country."

The U.S. Supreme Court school desegregation decision of 1954, voiding the old Plessy-Ferguson separate-but-equal doctrine, was a move toward clearing that unfinished business. Reactions to the decision varied throughout the Border region. Among the three former Confederate states, Virginia closed down two of its public school systems when confronted with desegregation. (One of these systems was in the highly urban concentration of Norfolk; the other was in the deeply rural county of Prince Edward.) These experiments at abandoning public education in favor of a prolonged recess for Negro children and improvised private schooling for white children were an alarming commentary on the state which had nurtured Thomas Jefferson and Woodrow Wilson.

In 1958, on the other hand, Greensboro, Charlotte and Winston-Salem, North Carolina, became the first school districts south of the Mason-Dixon line to begin voluntary desegregation.

Throughout the Border States there were advances and retreats in school desegregation, instances of peaceful adjustment and of violent reaction. One of the most publicized examples of the latter occurred in Clinton, Tennessee, in the fall of 1956. Clinton is an east Tennessee hill town on the fringes of the coal country, seven miles from the atomic city of Oak Ridge, which had previously and quietly desegregated its high school. Clinton, too, would probably have brought Negroes into its high school peaceably—except for the efforts of an itinerant racist from New Jersey named John Kasper, who stirred the latent fears and aroused the racial hostilities of a vocal segment of the community. When an Alabama agitator, Asa Carter, joined Kasper in haranguing meetings and organizing white citizens' groups, violence erupted and was quelled only by the national guard, called out by the governor. Not long afterward, a white Baptist minister, walking to school with the Negro children who had been threatened, was assaulted and beaten. The town reacted: segregation was rejected by the voters, and harassment of the school, its officials and its pupils declined. But the culminating episode of the ugly story was yet to come. Integrated Clinton High School was dynamited and destroyed. Citizens from many parts of the United States contributed to rebuilding the school—and the segregationist cause at Clinton High School was dead. John Kasper returned to the obscurity from which he had emerged so abruptly.

The victory at Clinton reflects larger conflicts and issues throughout the Border States, and indicates how some of them, at least, can be resolved by the ballot. In this area, Negroes, like whites, have a role to play, and the Negroes of the Border

States are active in politics as they have not been since Reconstruction. In Norfolk during a recent election, 30 per cent of the total vote was Negro although only 27 per cent of the population is Negro. One of the striking facts about Virginia, however, remains the low rate of voter participation by both races. In 1964, only 55.9 per cent of eligible white voters were registered, while the percentage for Negroes was even lower: 45.7.

Until the beginning of the 1960s, the major changes in the region's Negro-white relationships had been brought about by legal action, such as the repeal of Jim Crow laws. But laws and even the power of the ballot were limited in the changes they could effect and the pace at which these changes proceeded. A study of Durham, North Carolina, where Negroes have voted freely for many years and where a shift of Negro votes could have reversed two thirds of the mayoral races since 1945, showed that even in this progressive city there were sharp limits on what the vote could achieve for the Negro. In the words of the study report, "It did not effect any change in the strictly private sector, such as private housing; did not secure the integration of such facilities as parks, libraries, and schools; and perhaps played only a small role in developing public accommodations and gaining jobs for Negroes. Where Negro votes *did* have effect was in bringing more equitable distribution of funds for public facilities such as parks and street lights, opening municipal jobs, and halting police brutality."

As the power of the law and the vote failed to dispel all the barriers and indignities surrounding their lives, young Negroes launched their own revolution, a revolution that would sweep across the nation. Significantly it began in the Border States.

On Monday, February 1, 1960, at 4:30 in the afternoon, four freshmen enrolled at the Negro Agricultural and Technical College in Greensboro, North Carolina, sat down at the lunch counter of Greensboro's downtown Woolworth store. They ordered coffee and the waitress said, "I'm sorry, we don't serve colored here." The students sat waiting for service until the store closed at 5:30. The next day they returned.

Passive resistance to segregation had received a new impetus—and from that day until the present the resistance has intensified and widened to become a movement of massive proportions. Before that spring of 1960 was over every Southern state had experienced some demonstration of student resistance to segregation.

It was appropriate that the white and the Negro South finally met, morally and spiritually, in the Border States. This was where they had first met physically, 341 years earlier. Poised on their own border between total segregation and partial integration, Negroes made the Border States a frontier once again.

On this new frontier in the Border States myths have been crumbling fast: myths of Negro contentment and docility on the one hand, myths of Negro apathy and incapacity on the other. The skyline of Durham, North Carolina, is dominated by the 12-story concrete and glass tower of the North Carolina Mutual Building, home office of the largest Negro-owned and operated business in the world. There are Negro legislators who represent each of the three geographical divisions of Tennessee when the legislature meets in Nashville. In 1966 Kentucky approved the South's first statewide public accommodations law and in 1968 it passed the first statewide open housing law south of the Mason-Dixon line.

But the realities of Negro unemployment and underemployment, indignity and injustice, still plague the Border States no less than the rest of the country. Throughout the region, there are thousands of Negroes on the brink or in the abyss of failure. Among them are tenant farmers surviving on the remainders of the old plantations, welfare recipients clinging to a marginal existence—and, in one significant and fateful instance, urban garbage workers on strike for recognition of their union and for improved wages. The frustrations and unrest of this last group, in Memphis, were demonstrated in the spring of 1968, in a series of events that culminated in the tragic shooting of Dr. Martin Luther King Jr.

No event could have symbolized more powerfully the enduring division that still persists in the Border States. The divisions of slavery, of North against South and of East against West, of civil war—these had been resolved. But in other areas and issues—of education and housing and jobs, of equal rights and human respect—a division remained and a struggle continued. King's assassination dramatized that division and its importance to all the United States. For as one writer on the event, J. Edwin Stanfield, pointed out; "Memphis is America in microcosm. The sickness which led to the death of Dr. King can lead to the death of the United States. The only atonement for this murder, the only hope of national survival, is fast, full action to remedy the wrongs of racism."

Like any other boy, rich or poor, five-year-old Kenneth Doss breaks into a run as he leaves a Mingo County schoolhouse at the end of the day.

A rugged people's fight for life

Mingo County, West Virginia, has been called one of the richest treasuries of natural resources in the world. It is also one of the poorest places in the nation. Enormous wealth was extracted from the mountains around Mingo County, but little of that wealth has remained in the hands of its residents. Coal companies ripped into the mountains, reducing them from majestic wooded peaks to heaps of tailings and slag. When the mines were exhausted the companies moved out, taking their fortunes with them, and leaving only a few shabby buildings to the people of the area. Stripped of their sole means of support, these poverty-stricken but tough mountain people have turned to their only untapped resource—themselves —in a desperate attempt to bring independence and a decent standard of living to Mingo County.

Photographs by Michael Semak

81

An impoverished county's children

Bedecked in new dresses and hats, Debbie and Pamela York *(left)* attend an Easter service at Mingo County's Sprigg Freewill Baptist Church. The York family is poor—Mr. York earns $165 a month as a truck driver for an antipoverty project—but Debbie and Pamela, like most Mingo County children, do get new clothes every Easter.

Martha Jane Spencer, age five, plays with a hammer and nails on the front porch of her home. Martha Jane has few playthings, but she got a chance to hammer pegs into a pegboard as a pupil in Mingo County's Head Start program. At home, she dug into some of her father's tools, selected a hammer and nails, and began banging away.

Gathered around a potbellied stove (the wire screen protects them when the stove glows cherry red) Mingo County children at the Head Start school wait for their next activity to begin. As part of the Head Start program, 25 women took training courses at West Virginia University to prepare them for the task of educating the county's young citizens.

A county reshaped by "poor power"

In 1966, a group of Mingo County residents, concerned over the high price of food, opened their own cooperative grocery store. Within a week food prices dropped sharply at stores all over the county. Local merchants complained bitterly ("It's all a Communist plot," exclaimed one businessman), but Huey Perry, shown at top right addressing a group of local residents, has another word for such actions. He calls the cooperative grocery, which he aided with legal advice, an example of "poor power." Perry, a Mingo County native, is now executive director of the local antipoverty program. He argues that "it's important for the poor to mobilize their forces collectively." As a first step in this mobilization, Perry's office is tackling the county's most important problem, unemployment. Through his efforts ex-miners like James Curry *(bottom left)* and Buster Maynard *(bottom right)* have left the welfare lists and, with the help of government funds, are earning a living in such projects as the repair of neglected roads and the renovation of dilapidated schools. Other antipoverty activities include the programs of education and retraining shown on the following pages.

The road to
self-reliance

James Washington *(left)* and Okie Spencer *(right)* preside over a meeting of Mingo County's Fair Elections Committee. Opposing the county's old-line political machine, the committee has managed to clear the voter registration lists of more than 6,000 names, some of whose owners had been dead for more than 40 years.

John Blankenship, a 54-year-old ex-miner, has triumphantly written his own name under the direction of local schoolteacher Louise Smith. Out of work for so long that he was on the verge of starvation when he entered the antipoverty program, he is now an able carpenter and is learning to read and write in adult education classes.

Grover Maynard and his son Raymond work on a log cabin in Newsome Ridge Park, a 28-acre wilderness donated to the antipoverty program by a retired miner. Antipoverty workers have improved the property by digging wells and constructing cabins and barbecue pits in hope of attracting tourists to the area.

Mrs. Amanda Taylor teaches preschool-age children in a Mingo County Head Start center. Much of the classroom equipment, such as blocks, bookshelves and desks, was made in one of the antipoverty program's workshops, where the county's poor are taught new trades.

The question: survival

In a discussion of the future of Mingo County, retired miner Nemrod Workman speaks out at a community meeting. "The older kids have picked up and left," he says, "but now's the time for us to see that things are changed so that they might want to come back some day.... I want the kids to have a chance we didn't have."

To teenagers like Raymond Maynard *(left)* and Ralph Marcum, Mingo County offers an uncertain future. The antipoverty program has created a genuine hope for improvement, but it may fail to bring enough good jobs soon enough, and many of the county's young people may be forced to leave in search of better opportunities.

For Mrs. Russell Butler, mother of seven, the question of survival in Mingo County has been answered. Cuts in government appropriations reduced her husband's antipoverty salary from $265 to $165 per month, and the Butlers had to leave the county. They may become one more statistic in the record of West Virginia's dwindling population—or they may in time return to a resurgent Mingo County.

5

Industry in
a Rural Setting

Over the city of Richmond today, over the sprawl of Durham and the skyscrapers of commercial Winston-Salem, there often hangs a rich and heavy aroma, at times so heady that it seems to become visible in a golden light washed across the city buildings. It is the exotic smell of tobacco, aging, blending, rolling forth in rivers of cigarettes from the world's largest factories.

Over the rural-metropolitan paradox that is Louisville, there clings the mellow yet biting fragrance of whiskey aging in white oak barrels.

But across some of the towns clustered along inland Appalachian valleys there frequently drifts the acrid stench of chemicals and paper pulp as these 20th Century necessities pour out in steadily mounting streams from plants built half a century ago or only yesterday.

"It would seem," says one North Carolinian, "that the vices have more tempting aromas than the necessities. But pleasant or unpleasant they both smell like money to us."

These modern aromas have been displacing others that were once more familiar to the Border States—the scent of "new-turned" ground in spring and summer rain, of Winesap, Delicious and pippin apples ripening in autumn haze. This has been an essentially rural region reluctantly submitting to industrialization. Thus, the largest of its states, North Carolina, ranks second in the country in its number of small farms, while at the same time it has become one of the most industrialized states in the union. One of Virginia's most knowledgeable natives insists that Virginians *"work* in factories without fully *believing* in them," without endorsing them emotionally—yet in Virginia today, manufacturing provides jobs for almost three times as many workers as does agriculture.

Virginians were almost forced to believe in factories during the Civil War, when there were so few factories and so desperate a need for them. An example of the essential and cherished factories of that period was the Tredegar Iron Works in Richmond. During the Civil War, Tredegar's owner became one of the few men ever drafted *out* of an army—so that he might bring the production of his factory to maximum capacity.

Never again would the importance of industry be minimized in the Border States; it might be

Tobacco farmer Arthur Williard inspects his ripening crop near Winston-Salem, North Carolina, choosing leaves ready for picking. After drying and curing the leaves, Williard will sell them at auction to the region's cigarette producers.

deplored by those who preferred the rural way of life, but never underestimated. In the century following the Civil War, the wheels of industrialization would roll with increasing power and productivity across the Border States.

The raw materials for industrialization existed in plenty throughout the region, for natural resources of immense richness stretched from the Atlantic to the Ohio and to the Mississippi. There were far-flung forests of pine and hardwood, untapped billions of tons of coal, land containing a variety of industrial clays and loams and sands, vast deposits of rock-salt and other minerals. There was abundant water, available for power plants in mighty rivers and innumerable cataracts. Above all, there was the resource of people—of manpower, muscle and brain—ready for a new era.

Nevertheless, despite all this raw wealth, the Border States were desperately poor in the years immediately following the Civil War. Like the backwoods soldier during the war who explained that he was eating green persimmons to draw in his stomach to fit his rations, the region had to shrink its needs to a devastated economy. Its land was neglected; its smokehouses, corncribs, barns and root cellars were bare; cities were prostrate under a pall of dust and despair; rail lines were in disrepair; even fences were demolished, consumed in the campfires of two armies. Cash was scarce and credit slim. Newly freed but hopelessly unprepared Negroes, who had never before managed their own affairs, were roaming the countryside. Only confusion flourished. By the end of Reconstruction, in 1877, the overriding question was: How could the region become part of the national economy and prosperity?

Paradoxically, clues indicating how the problem would eventually be met, if not solved, appeared in Northern newspapers. In July 1877, the Philadelphia *Evening Telegraph* enthusiastically proclaimed that in the South "land, labor, fuel, water power, and building facilities are cheap. The way to clear and large profits is open." Northern capital would conquer and transform the Border States more fundamentally than the war itself had done, and those who had been fighting against the Yankees were now fighting over the Yankees, eager for a new invasion.

Some parts of the region were aggressive in their eagerness to join the national progress. In December 1868, for example, Chattanooga advertised that it wished to "extend a GENERAL INVITATION to all CARPET-BAGGERS to leave the bleak winds of the North" and come to Tennessee. Partly through such appeals, the city boosted itself from a population of some 3,500 at the start of the Civil War to 30,000 by the turn of the century.

In still other parts of the Border States, such as Kentucky, men found other ways to lift themselves by their bootstraps. There, a home-grown—or, more accurately perhaps, home-brewed—industry grew as naturally as bluegrass from the native roots and folklore of the region; today it continues to influence the economy of a part of the Border States and the social tastes of the U.S.

Since colonial days, the region had been involved in manufacturing whiskey. A distillery, or still, was considered as essential on the frontier as a sawmill or a gristmill. By 1783, five years after George Rogers Clark planted a settlement for 11 families at the site of Louisville, Kentucky, whiskey was being manufactured there in quantity.

Significantly, the very word "whiskey" was probably first used to designate a drink made in Scotland and Ireland. As Scotch-Irish settlers flooded the Border States during the great migrations of colonial times, they brought with them both a powerful thirst and the recipe for its satisfaction. Harriette Simpson Arnow, who grew up in the Cumberland River country, says, "Whiskey was to the pioneer what tranquilizers, stimulants, disinfectants, vitamins, rubbing alcohol, and anaesthetics are to us today. The newborn got weak toddy at birth, the mother had it stronger, the father straight, the old and cold bathed their limbs in it." What was perhaps more important, whiskey was also a valuable cash "crop" for the pioneer farmer.

The primary reason, perhaps, for the early growth of the whiskey industry in the Border States lay in a problem of transportation. Cleared forest lands produced lavish yields of corn. (Before the Civil War, Tennessee was called the Hog and Hominy State in recognition of its position as a leading corn producer in the Union.) But getting a crop of corn to Eastern markets over mountain trails was a hard, costly job, and a packhorse that could carry four bushels of corn as grain could carry 24 bushels of corn as whiskey. The same held true for shipping by water. Whiskey sent down the Ohio to New Orleans and around Cape Horn to California helped to enliven the Gold Rush days there. (It may also have contributed to the fact that California is the biggest bourbon market in the United States today.)

It is agreed that the limestone-rich water of Kentucky is a basic ingredient of good bourbon, but there is no agreement as to when the first bourbon was concocted or who introduced the charred white oak that imparts its special color and flavor. One tradition credits a Baptist minister, the Reverend Elijah Craig, with first making the whiskey in 1789, when he accidentally charred some staves he was heating for making barrels. Thriftily, Craig used the burned staves anyway—and discovered that the whiskey he aged in these barrels was of a different, and a better, quality than any he had turned out before. Today, according to federal regulations, every one of the 96 million gallons of bourbon produced annually in the Border States must be stored at least two years in new charred oak barrels. Obviously cooperage is a major industry in bourbon country.

Despite its early manufacture and heavy consumption in the Border States, whiskey has always produced an ambivalent reaction among the people there. From the time of the first saddlebag preachers to sophisticated present-day campaigns against legalized alcoholic beverages, strong opposition to the making, selling and drinking of whiskey has existed alongside the profitable commerce in it at all these levels. There may be some symbolism in the fact that Kentucky gave birth both to prohibitionist Carry Nation and to bourbon whiskey. North Carolina never ratified the 21st Amendment, repealing prohibition—but in 1966 agents of the U.S. Alcohol and Tobacco Tax Office destroyed 1,095 illegal North Carolinian stills capable of producing millions of gallons of whiskey. As cynical residents of some "dry" enclaves of the region mutter, "Methodists, Baptists and moonshiners keep us the driest-voting and the wettest-drinking section of the country today."

A greater challenge to Kentucky than prohibitionist sentiment is a constantly changing public taste. In 1949 two competing beverages, gin and vodka, had slightly more than 2 per cent of the American market; today they have nearly 20 per cent. But the home of the mint julep and the distillation of corn cannot believe that the call for "bourbon and branch water" will ever be displaced. And the Border States' annual production of 106 million gallons of whiskey (the national total is 140 million gallons) still makes the industry an influential force in the region.

It is no longer, however, a dominant force. Even in Kentucky, only 3.5 per cent of all manufacturing workers are employed in the liquor industry today. New industries have assumed commanding positions throughout the Border States, and the sounds of the new era began rising during the latter part of the 19th Century, when Northern industrialists and financiers began to exploit the region's resources.

Some of these sounds came from an old and familiar uproar of axe and saw. Drivers of oxen, mules and horses logged valleys and hills that contained some of the largest stands of virgin hardwoods in the United States. They logged stands of timber scattered from the Little Kanawha Lumber Company (a Maine corporation) in West Virginia to the forests of East Tennessee—where one native hailed the "investments of Northern capital. . . . We welcome the skilled lumberman with the noisy mill." West Virginia sawed more lumber in 1909 than it ever would produce again: almost 1,500 million board-feet of oak, chestnut, yellow poplar, hemlock, maple and other woods. All across the Border States the trees fell in an orgy of cutting, burning, slashing.

There was also the din of miners heaving coal from the underground darkness and sending it to stoke the fires of a rapidly industrializing nation. Dingy, monotonous mining towns sprang up in West Virginia, Kentucky and southwest Virginia; coal tipples and growing mountains of slag blighted the landscape. From 16 million tons of coal produced in West Virginia in 1898, the quantity mounted to almost 67 million tons in 1912.

The swaying clank and rattle of the railroad cars that carried this coal also resounded across the region and sped the process of industrialization. Before the turn of the century the Norfolk and Western Railway began pouring such quantities of coal into Norfolk that the city became the greatest coal port in the world. And along the railroad lines, there were the noises of construction as country crossroads became towns, and villages grew into cities.

Another sound of the time was the ring of rails being adjusted to the narrower standard gauge used in the North. For years, the three-inch difference in width between Northern and Southern railways had resulted in delays and inconvenience at the Potomac and Ohio River boundaries of the Border States. Now the railway systems were welded into one. At the same time, the ownership of the railroads was consolidated in the hands of Northern financiers. Historian C. Vann Woodward describes the change in his *Origins of the New South*: "Northeastern control over the vast, sprawling railway system of the South was virtually completed within the decade following the

The Border States' own brew

Bourbon, the native whiskey of the Border States, is made by the process beginning at right. Grains (at least 51 per cent corn) are ground, then mixed with germinated barley malt in a pressure cooker called a mash tank, where the grains' starch becomes fermentable sugar. As the mash ferments with sour mash, made from fresh yeast and "spent beer," liquid left over from a previous fermentation, the sugar becomes alcohol. A still vaporizes the alcohol along with certain other grain substances called congeners, leaving a residue of spent beer at the bottom; then a condenser cools the vapor to a liquid. This freshly made whiskey is aged in charred oak barrels *(tan shade, below),* then sold as is or blended with other whiskeys or grain neutral spirits (nearly pure alcohol, indicated by beige-colored barrels below).

THE PROCESS

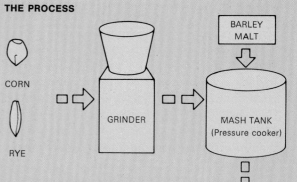

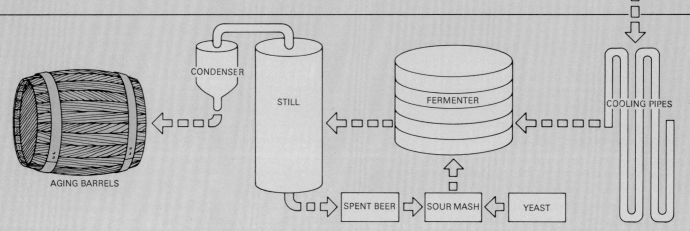

THE PRODUCTS

BOURBON WHISKEY
(Rarely marketed as such.)

Aged less than 2 years.
Bottled at less than 80 proof.

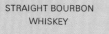

STRAIGHT BOURBON
WHISKEY

Aged 2 or more years.
Bottled at not less than 80 proof,
customarily at 86 proof.

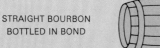

STRAIGHT BOURBON
BOTTLED IN BOND

Aged 4 or more years.
Bottled at 100 proof
as so attested by U.S. Government.

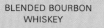

BLENDED STRAIGHT
BOURBON WHISKEY

At least 2 straight bourbon whiskeys.
Aged 2 or more years.
Customarily bottled at 86 proof.

BLENDED BOURBON
WHISKEY

At least 51% straight bourbon
whiskey aged 2 or more years.
Plus 49% or less grain neutral spirits
or other whiskey not necessarily aged.
Customarily bottled at 86 proof.

SPIRIT BLEND
(BLENDED) WHISKEY

At least 20% 100-proof straight bourbon
whiskey aged 2 or more years.
Plus 80% or less grain neutral spirits.
Customarily bottled at 80 to 86 proof.

Panic of 1893 by a series of large-scale reorganizations. J. Pierpont Morgan, mightiest of the Northern empire builders, opened the era of reorganization and consolidation by creating the Southern Railway out of the ruins of the Richmond and West Point Terminal Company in 1894." Similarly, control and ownership of the important Louisville and Nashville Railroad passed into Northern hands, and among those directing its destiny (and that of Kentucky itself, to a large extent) were such tycoons as Jay Gould, Thomas Fortune Ryan and Russell Sage.

There was also the hum of cotton mills, mainly in the Piedmont—and here, too, Northern capital was moving in. A few mills had been in existence before the Civil War; from them came a core of experienced textile workers, native managers and some owners who could lead in the postwar growth. By 1898, when Northern influence was reaching its height, the North Carolina Bureau of Labor Statistics could declare that the state had become "the Massachusetts of the South." At the turn of the century North Carolina had 177 cotton mills, employing more than 30,000 workers and producing goods valued at $28,000,000.

Along with other contributing factors, the overriding consideration that attracted the exploitive capital of the North was—people. The Arkwright Club, an association of New England textile manufacturers, reported that "labor is cheaper in the South; that the hours of labor are longer, and that there is neither any of the restrictive legislation urged among us by the labor unions." The cost of labor was 40 per cent lower in the South than in New England, and the working day in North Carolina was 24 per cent longer than in Massachusetts. Up to 1906 the average work week in North Carolina was 69 hours. (The stereotype of the work-shy Southerner fades away before such statistical evidence of the work-worn Southerner.) The disparities between the Border States and their neighbors to the North would eventually diminish but never disappear; the lures of cheap labor and few unions have continued to draw Northern capital for the textile and other industries until the present day.

Yet the Northerners did not have it all their own way. Alongside efforts to lure outside capital, many citizens of the Border States campaigned for an economy financed and owned within the region. In 1880, for example, the *News and Observer* of Raleigh, North Carolina, addressed an impassioned question to North Carolinians: "What

nobler employment could enlist the energies of a people than developing the great resources of our God-favoured States, and having it possessed and enjoyed by an enlightened, law-abiding, peaceful people? But with all its varied and splendid capabilities, it is idle to talk of home independence so long as we go to the North for everything from a toothpick to a President."

At that moment, in the neighboring town of Durham, one native son was just beginning to flex his muscle. His life and the industry he built in his own image epitomize the energies of the Border States in both agriculture and industry. Indeed, the rise of James Buchanan Duke and the tobacco empire he created might stand as a parable of much of the contemporary Border States' history, which is also an integral part of America's history. In this latter-day instance, however, the Border States' contribution is not that of a Virginia dynasty of political leaders but a North Carolina dynasty of industrial giants.

"Buck Duke," Vann Woodward has said, "was no empire builder from the Northeast. He came right out of the colony." Moreover, he came out of one of the poorest of the colonies. In 1900 the estimated value of tangible wealth in North Carolina was only $360 per capita—a little more than half that of Virginia or Kentucky, and about three quarters as much as that of Tennessee. By history and attitude, North Carolinians were a plain people who took pride in not being proud, in their state motto—"To be rather than to seem"—and in what one of their judges once called a "militant mediocracy."

In his origins, at least, James Duke belonged completely to that world. Discussing the Dukes with journalist Jonathan Daniels, a Durham politician said, "They were common people. The Dukes weren't just plain. They were common." To which Daniels' reply was that the Dukes may have robbed their state or they may have enriched it, but "the certain thing is that they changed it more than any other people ever did before—or since."

The robbery, the enrichment and the change were all founded on tobacco. Tobacco had saved Jamestown, the first weakling colony of the Border States and America, by providing it with a profitable agricultural staple; now it would help to save a tottering economy by providing it with a wholly new industry. The crop that had sustained the plantation aristocracy of Virginia became the foundation of half a dozen powerful corporations,

95

created the first native millionaires in the post-Civil War scramble for survival, and produced vast stores of capital for the development of other regional resources.

During colonial days and long afterward, North Carolina tobacco was considered inferior to that of Virginia. But in 1839 Abisha Slade's slave Stephen built a charcoal fire in the Caswell County barn where Slade's tobacco crop was curing. As the heat mounted, Slade discovered that the aroma improved and the color of the big leaves turned to a golden yellow. The subsequent development of flue-curing (that is, curing by artificial heat rather than natural air curing) revolutionized tobacco growing. It made so-called Bright Leaf tobacco, especially adapted to the light, sandy soil of North Carolina's Piedmont, the dominant variety on the market. And in so doing, it tumbled Virginia from its leadership in tobacco growing and manufacture and placed North Carolina in permanent supremacy.

Uses of tobacco were altering radically, too. Pipes had been in use since the days of the Indians and Sir Walter Raleigh and John Rolfe. Chewing tobacco was also popular with many colonists and from them sailors (who were often forbidden to smoke aboard the wooden ships of the time) picked up the habit and spread it around the globe. Gradually, chewing tobacco leaves had given way to a backwoods innovation called "plug" tobacco. In the backwoods, a few tobacco leaves were saturated with wild honey and apple or peach brandy and wedged into a hole bored in a green hickory or maple log. After the log was dry the potent dark-brown "plug" was removed. And there were many country men who believed (and many who still believe, in remote corners of the Border States) that those who smoked tobacco could never know its flavor as did those who savored a bite from a well-cured plug.

At one time there were more than 12,000 brands of chewing tobacco on the market, including 200 whose names began with "Big" and another large number whose names began with "Honest." Still other names included Mule Ear and Jaw Bone, and such flights of fancy as Otto of Roses and Darling Fanny Pan Cake.

More exotic forms of tobacco were slower to catch on. Cigars, which came into favor in America in the early 1800s, required a special sort of tobacco and a hand-rolling process of considerable skill; the best ones came from semitropical regions, such as Cuba, and only the stronger, cheap-er grades were made from U.S. tobacco. Cigarettes were originally smoked in Russia and Turkey and were introduced to England and France by soldiers who fought in the Crimean War of 1854-1856. Some Americans began to smoke imported cigarettes soon afterward, but the real cigarette revolution did not begin until the turn of the century.

The Civil War slowed tobacco growing, but not its use. In fact, the war increased the demand for whiskey and tobacco, both of them indigenous to the Border States. And there were bold, shrewd men ready to seize upon the tobacco boom and ride it as far as it could be pushed, pulled, squeezed, thrust or finagled—which was right into our own time.

The first to grasp his opportunity when it came was a Durham tobacco manufacturer and merchant named John Ruffin Green. When the Confederate and Union Armies made the war's last skirmishes and final peace in the vicinity of Durham, they raided Green's tobacco warehouse. Green appeared to be ruined. But when the soldiers returned home, they began to send orders to Durham for more of "Mr. Green's tobacco." They liked the distinctive flavor of North Carolina Bright Leaf. Business revived.

John Green happily filled the orders, but he soon realized he needed a distinctive trademark to keep customers ordering his tobacco rather than that of numerous Durham competitors. When a friend suggested the combination of a picture of a bull with the name of the city, one of the world's best known tobaccos—and the earliest of all "saturation advertising" campaigns—was launched. "Bull Durham" tobacco became one of America's first products to make extensive use of the testimonials of prominent people and to advertise the names of famous users. The manufacturers let it be known that Thomas Carlyle and James Russell Lowell and Alfred Lord Tennyson used Bull Durham. The big black bull appeared on signs from New England to the Pacific, in Europe, and even on one of the pyramids in Egypt. At the home plant, a huge steam whistle was used to imitate the bellow of a bull ("Each bellow," according to one authority, "cost six dollars and could be clearly heard thirteen miles away"). And from that plant poured a flood of tobacco—not the pallid, filter-tipped "readymade" cigarettes now named Bull Durham, but robust chewing tobacco, pipe tobacco, and the "makings" for "roll-your-owns."

Meanwhile, on a 300-acre farm near Durham,

an even more important company was in its infancy. In 1865 Washington Duke, a 45-year-old widower who had walked 137 miles home after being mustered out of the Confederate Army, found himself with 50 cents cash, a small quantity of Bright Leaf tobacco, a daughter, Mary, and three young sons: Brodie Lawrence, Benjamin Newton and James Buchanan, or "Buck." In a little log storage barn, Washington Duke, with 10-year-old Ben and 9-year-old Buck, pulverized the tobacco, sifted it and packed it in bags bearing the label "Pro Bono Publico." Then they hitched their two blind mules to a wagon loaded with the tobacco and enough food for a journey—sweet potatoes, a side of bacon, a bushel of meal—and hauled their tobacco to eastern North Carolina, where they sold it readily.

The next year they planted and pulverized and peddled tobacco again, and a 20-by-30-foot log factory was added to the farm. Later, in 1873, Washington Duke moved his factory from the farm into a three-story frame building in Durham. Buck took a six-month course at the Eastman School of Business in Poughkeepsie, New York, and came home ready to make his way in the industrial world. When he was 18 he was made a full partner of W. Duke & Sons.

This was the unlikely beginning of the most remarkable business career in the Border States: the rise of the only Southern colossus of finance who could compare with John D. Rockefeller. Soon afterward, according to his own recollection, James Buchanan Duke compared himself with the Standard Oil tycoon: "I said to myself, 'If John D. Rockefeller can do what he is doing for oil, why should not I do it in tobacco?'" And though the lanky, red-haired, pigeon-toed farm boy may not have addressed himself in exactly that language, the energy behind his words was exactly that bold and aggressive.

In 1881 Buck Duke made one of the great decisions of his career. His company would manufacture cigarettes. That year, two million pounds of Bull Durham were sold; chewing tobacco dominated the market. Nevertheless, Duke brought 10 Russian and Polish Jews to Durham to teach his own workers, many of them Negroes, how to roll cigarettes by hand. But while Duke was trying to persuade reluctant dealers to handle cigarettes, while he was hiring salesmen and launching an ambitious advertising campaign, a momentous development was taking place in Virginia. A young man named James Bonsack was perfecting a cig-

arette-making machine. In 1883, Duke ordered some of Bonsack's experimental machines; after they arrived in Durham, he discovered that with minor improvements, a single machine could roll as many cigarettes a day as 50 expert handrollers. The machines cut the cost of manufacture by more than half, and gave Duke a big edge in a new tobacco market.

The following year Duke left North Carolina for New York City, then the center of the infant cigarette industry. He installed four Bonsack machines in a loft on Rivington Street and began making cigarettes there. At the same time, he also launched a nationwide advertising campaign for his machine-made cigarettes. Posters blossomed with invitations to try a cigarette. Pictures of national flags and of famous actresses or athletes were included in the packages. ("That was a million-dollar idea," recalled one veteran New York tobacco dealer, "for the pictures came in numbered sets and the kids began pestering their dads for them. Soon collecting pictures became a craze and we had to order [Duke's] cigarettes in quantity.") And above all else there was Buck Duke himself, prowling the city streets to visit dealers and small shop owners. A rugged Tar Heel red-neck was showing New York what work and imagination could accomplish. He spent 12 hours a day in his plant—and in his off hours he bought, sold, chewed, spat, talked, thought and dreamed tobacco.

When Buck Duke came onto the national scene there were four major cigarette manufacturers, one in Richmond and three in New York State. They scorned their back-country competitor, whom they considered more of a mountebank than a manufacturer—but within three years they had begun to realize their mistake. By 1889 Duke was making more than half again as many cigarettes as the biggest of them. When he called his rivals together and suggested formation of one company, they reluctantly agreed. The American Tobacco Company was incorporated in 1890, with Duke as its president. It held a 90 per cent monopoly on all cigarette manufacturing in the United States.

But Americans were still buying twice as much plug tobacco as cigarette tobacco. Duke had cigarettes firmly under control. Now he—or, more precisely, the American Tobacco Company— purchased a Louisville, Kentucky, plug-tobacco company, which gave him leverage in that field. In succession, snuff, pipe tobacco and cigar companies were acquired. When associates in Ameri-

James Buchanan "Buck" Duke, founder of the powerful American Tobacco Company, applied high-pressure business techniques to North Carolina's tobacco industry and developed the cigarette from an exotic rarity to the common man's everyday smoke.

can who objected to the new policy of diversification tried to out-maneuver Duke and gain control of the company, they found themselves out of the business.

Fierce price wars in plug tobacco were waged, especially with P. Lorillard Company and Liggett & Myers. American took deep cuts in its cigarette profits to entrench itself in other markets. Secret rebates, under-the-counter deals, every trick of cut-throat marketing came into play. And in the end, Duke won. In 1898 the huge Continental Tobacco Company was formed with Buck Duke as its president and dominant figure. It included five big chewing and smoking tobacco firms. Taken together, Continental Tobacco and Duke's own American Tobacco Company constituted the Tobacco Trust, dominating the tobacco industry and ready to move into the distribution of tobacco products.

The road to Continental Tobacco had been marked by many a milestone. There was symbolism in Duke's absorption of the old company that had manufactured Bull Durham—and its prompt dissolution as a North Carolina corporation. And there was prophecy in the acquisition of a plug-tobacco empire controlled by a fellow North Carolinian, R. J. Reynolds. "If Buck Duke

tries to swallow me, he'll get the bellyache of his life," Reynolds warned. The trust did swallow him for a time. It did not digest him. He had his own mark to make in the tobacco world.

During this catalytic period of the industry's growth, those who produced the tobacco—farmers who, tradition said, spent 13 months a year raising one of the most demanding crops that grows—were the last to profit and the first to lose in each market's rise and fall. The Bright Leaf country of North Carolina and the Burley growing region of Tennessee and Kentucky were the two areas most sensitive to manipulation and control of prices. And eventually the power of the Tobacco Trust led to one of the most tragic episodes of the Border States' history. It was called the Black Patch War.

The Black Patch is the area of Kentucky and Tennessee where dark-leaf tobacco is grown. In 1904, after years of overproduction, the Tobacco Trust forced the price for dark tobacco down and down until it was lower than the cost of growing it, and the desperate farmers reacted by forming the Dark Tobacco District Planters' Protective Association. The association sought to improve prices by various appeals and pressures (particularly boycotts) on the trust. When such methods failed, small extremist groups within the protective association began to form. These so-called Night Riders were vigilantes who intimidated farmers who would not join the association or participate in its boycotts.

Factories belonging to the trust were dynamited; warehouses and railroad stations were burned. Homes and barns of nonmembers of the association were razed; independent farmers were whipped, and sometimes murdered. Plant beds were scraped, so that many farmers were left without means for growing their tobacco crop in the coming season. The Night Riders even took temporary possession of two western Kentucky towns. As one resident later recalled, "neighbor suspected neighbor. Openly or secretly the bulk of the Black Patch people were armed for conflict. Since about the beginning of 1906, town after town had been raided, building after building burnt or shattered. Fire insurance, bond and loan companies had withdrawn from the district."

As it turned out, however, the Night Riders' power lasted only a couple of years. By the end of 1908 their terrorism had been curbed by military force; what was more important, dark tobacco prices improved.

And as for Buck Duke, the terror on the land

had little connection with his life in New York. He had come from the land, but the farm was far behind him now. In addition to controlling the major part of the nation's tobacco industry, he was promoting one of the first major chain-store organizations in America as a controlled market for his products. The Whelan brothers' United Cigar Stores Company, dominated by the trust, eventually grew to 2,500 brightly decorated, highly organized stores across the United States and Canada.

John Winkler describes the effects of this sales monopoly: "As the Trust, through its retail satellite, spread its tentacles from city to city and from state to state, public bitterness against the monopoly and its master increased tremendously. The methods by which rival retailers were driven out of business was one of the few operations of the Trust that were visible to the eyes of the laymen. The least observant noted the disappearance of the little independent dealer soon after the big, glittering Trust store was set up on the next corner. And there were personal tragedies involved that could not be hidden: the distress of old men, invalids, cripples, Civil War veterans, whose one source of livelihood was their small shops."

Four fifths of the U.S. tobacco industry exclusive of cigars was controlled by the trust—but the trust also enjoyed the country's bitterness and enmity. And though the trust might have managed to ignore the Black Patch farmers and the small store owners, even it could not defy all the nation's people—particularly at a time when the nation was led by the greatest trust-buster of them all, President Theodore Roosevelt.

In May 1908, the Raleigh *News and Observer* carried a headline: "Teddy About to Jump onto Buck." Three years later, by a unanimous decision of the United States Supreme Court, the Tobacco Trust was ordered dissolved. Eventually, the trust was not so much dissolved as divided. In 1912 it was broken up into four separate companies— Liggett & Myers, P. Lorillard, R. J. Reynolds and American Tobacco.

When R. J. Reynolds heard of the decision ordering the break-up of the trust, he exulted: "Now watch me give Buck Duke hell!" War and women helped him keep his promise. In 1916 Americans smoked 25.2 billion cigarettes. By 1919 the number had more than doubled, to 53.1 billion. The tensions of World War I and a new emancipation for women had been major causes of that growth. And riding the crest of this wave was an R. J. Reynolds cigarette blended of Bright

Richard Joshua Reynolds, "Buck" Duke's fiercest competitor, introduced the first modern American cigarette, Camel, to the public in 1913. Reynolds himself named the new brand and planned the advertising campaigns that led to its success.

Leaf, Burley and Turkish tobaccos—the first light-colored cigarette of a new American type (earlier blends, the dark-colored, so-called Turkish cigarettes, had been more pungent in flavor and aroma), pushed by one of the most formidable advertising campaigns Americans had yet experienced, and labeled by the short, exotic name of Camel. ("Tomorrow there will be more Camels in this town than in all Asia and Africa," one ad boasted.) In 1919 nearly 40 per cent of the cigarettes sold in America were Camels.

Reynolds' leadership in the field was not fleeting. Today, in the R. J. Reynolds Tobacco Company's sleek modern building, three miles from the center of Winston-Salem, the world's largest cigarette factory turns out 187 billion cigarettes a year: Winstons, the nation's best-selling brand, Salems, and Camels, still the most popular unfiltered cigarette.

Despite Camels, and Reynolds' growth, Buck Duke was not in hell. He went on to other big undertakings, and two of the most significant of them were in the Border States.

During the years following World War I, Duke applied his still enormous energies (he was then in his sixties) to the development of the Border States' untapped hydroelectric power. In the Carolina Piedmont, he built up the Duke Power Company, which he had acquired as early as 1905. By 1930 its potential output of 695,000 horsepower gave Duke Power, according to one observer, the capacity to produce more energy than all the slaves of the Old South.

With power available, Duke began to invest in textile mills using his power. As a result, Duke Power was soon serving more than one third of all the spindles in the southern United States.

James Buchanan Duke's final monument was not fully completed till many years after his death —and in one sense of the word will never be "completed" at all. Small, struggling Methodist Trinity College had been a beneficiary of Washington Duke's philanthropy, and in 1922 his son gave the school one million dollars. When Buck learned, a while later, that the institution would change its name to Duke University if a larger gift were made, he added another six million dollars. Eventually, he created the Duke Endowment, with funds of more than $80 million, and a large part of its income to go to the University. (During its first 25 years, the Endowment turned over more than $95 million to the school.) Thus, the handsome neo-Gothic stone buildings of the "Ivy League college of the South," Duke University, came into being.

Washington Duke once said of his son, "You know, there are three things I just can't seem to understand: ee-lec-tricity, the Holy Ghost, and my son Buck." But Buck understood what he was doing. He stood astride the border between the old rural South and the new industrialized South. It is significant that in merging companies and forging an empire he depended most heavily for assistance on men with rural backgrounds. (He himself once said, "The country boy can come to town and soon learn all the town boy knows. But the town boy can never get all that the country boy has had.") Of three great North Carolina industries—tobacco, textiles and furniture—he helped create one and gave decisive impetus to another. He left as his namesake one of the country's foremost universities. And he bequeathed both riches and problems to the Border States.

Tobacco is still Kentucky's principal agricultural crop. In 1966 tobacco crowded out cotton as Tennessee's leading crop. And North Carolina still grows more Bright Leaf and produces more cigarettes (nearly two thirds of all those made in the United States) than any other state. North Carolina pays more money in excise taxes to the federal government than any of the other states except Michigan and New York—and it is the tobacco industry that pays it.

But recent medical findings on the relationship between smoking and such ailments as cancer and heart disease have presented the Border States with a challenge. Their agricultural and industrial economy relies too heavily on the golden weed. The big tobacco companies are diversifying; they are intensifying efforts to expand overseas markets, where they feel their growth potential is much greater than in this country; and they are expanding their own research on the hazards of smoking. For the moment, however, despite health warnings of individual and government doctors, medical experiments and cancer prevention societies, the American public shows little sign of giving up its cigarettes.

The tobacco industry's dilemma, however it comes to be resolved, is only one of the Border States' industrial problems. Far more grave is the problem of low wages throughout the region, a problem that is highlighted in the pattern of industrial wages in Buck Duke's home state of North Carolina.

In a report issued in June 1967, the North Carolina Fund, a non-profit research and program-development organization, pointed out some facts which gave progressive North Carolinians pause for thought. One fact: North Carolina was 43rd in the nation in per capita income. (Kentucky was 44th; Tennessee, 45th; West Virginia, 46th. Virginia—the only state to break the Border States pattern—was 30th.) In three of North Carolina's major industries, tobacco workers' average hourly wage in the period from 1960 to 1965 was $2.21; furniture workers averaged $1.77 an hour; and textile workers, $1.78.

Industrial wages in North Carolina are among the lowest in the nation. Yet North Carolina has more of its work force (almost one third) in manufacturing than the country as a whole (which averages about one fourth). In 1965, North Carolina tied with Mississippi for last place among the 50 states ranked by average hourly earnings of production workers in manufacturing industries. And one of the facts of greatest concern to those trying to build up the state's real wealth was that, in each year since 1960, two thirds of the new manufacturing jobs created in North Carolina have been in industries paying less than the state's average wage for that year.

The Fund report pointed out: "Current eco-

100

nomic development policy relies heavily on industrialization as a means to increase income in North Carolina. Yet, while this policy has been in effect we have seen North Carolina shift from a poor agricultural state to a poor industrial state. We have experienced industrialization without development."

Buck Duke and his fellow visionary-realists and buccaneer-philanthropists, who set the wheels of the 20th Century spinning across the Border States, did not solve the region's real problems. It sometimes seems, in fact, that in meeting one problem they created two more. They cut the timber, mined the land, spun the thread, developed the machines, employed the people—yet the region still has to run in order to stand still by national standards. The paradoxical era of industrialization, with its forward thrust and its backward tug, has still to prove its value to the Border States.

One achievement of the region, however, an achievement that has been called "a massive monument of economic growth and development," illustrates industrialization of another kind. It is the Tennessee Valley Authority. Like a domestic Marshall Plan, the TVA helped an underdeveloped land to heal the gullies in its eroding soil, harness the power it needed for industrial productivity, and diminish the gap between the potential and the real.

This bold experiment was not the product of any single imagination or of any single doctrinaire program. It was born only after years of controversy, and it finally took a war and a depression to get it delivered. During World War I, the federal government started construction of the Wilson Dam and two nitrate munitions plants on the wild and treacherous Muscle Shoals rapids of the Tennessee River in northwest Alabama. For 15 years after the war a debate raged over the disposal of these plants. Of several offers to relieve the government of these properties, the one that came closest to being accepted was made by Henry Ford, who hoped to develop manufacturing facilities there—but some politicians insisted that the acceptance of Ford's proposal would be a virtual giveaway of government lands and property. Senator George W. Norris of Nebraska, for example, argued that handing over Muscle Shoals to Ford would constitute "the greatest gift ever bestowed upon mortal man since salvation was made free to the human race."

Senator Norris had a larger vision. He wanted Muscle Shoals to be operated for the public wel-fare, and eventually he found a President and a Congress to agree with him. On April 10, 1933, in the depths of the Depression, President Franklin D. Roosevelt sent a message to the Congress. It began with these words: "The continued idleness of a great national investment in the Tennessee Valley leads me to ask the Congress for legislation necessary to enlist this project in the service of the people."

The President pointed out that the existing facilities at Muscle Shoals represented only a token of the full development of the Tennessee River Valley. Beyond a single dam and two munitions factories, there lay the possibility of vast power production, of incalculable aid to agriculture and of the creation of diverse industries. "In short," the President said, "this power development of war days leads logically to national planning for a complete river watershed involving many States and the future lives and welfare of millions." And Roosevelt continued his message with a calm but pregnant proposal: "I, therefore, suggest to the Congress legislation to create a Tennessee Valley Authority." He called for the harnessing of a mighty river for flood control and navigation and the development of its watershed through land reclamation and power production.

Before the creation of the TVA, the Tennessee Valley was the most poverty-stricken major river basin in the United States. In 1929, annual personal income averaged $317, only 45 per cent of the national average. Fifteen of its counties had not a single manufacturing plant. It is not surprising that the support of the valley's people was a major factor in TVA's success and endurance. One analyst found that this support "was more intense and I think more understanding than that found in most river basins, where too often the pork barrel has been substituted for the cracker barrel as a symbol of local democracy." And in almost every respect, the TVA has fulfilled its promise.

TVA dams made the Tennessee River and its tributaries navigable for 750 miles. This led to complexes of industry that have transformed stretches of desolate riverfront into busy ports and factory developments. In 1967, 21.6 million tons of commercial freight traffic traveled on the Tennessee. Savings to shippers from this waterborne traffic, as opposed to other forms of transport, were estimated at $35.4 million.

The success of TVA's flood control program has been dramatized in many violent seasons. From its completion in 1936, Norris Dam prevented the Tennessee from joining the swirling Ohio and Mississippi in full flood. Since then, in projects extending from the largest dams to the smallest tributaries, the river's rampages have been controlled. If this achievement has tended to be underestimated over the years, it may be because, as one resident of the valley has said, *"Not* having a flood never grabs the headlines. You can't have pictures of a town *not* under water, and have them make news."

The Muscle Shoals installations of TVA now include the nation's chief center for fertilizer research. With famine a major threat to all mankind, this center is of vital interest throughout the world. At the request of the Agency for International Development, TVA specialists went to nine nations in 1967 to help plan soil improvement and fertilization projects. And on America's own farms, partly as a result of the kind of research carried on at Muscle Shoals, the only large farm expense that has not risen in recent years is the cost of fertilizer.

Other results of TVA, from its forestry programs to the boom in recreation on the lakes, have changed the face and habits of the region. In 1967 the area of reforested land in the valley passed the one-million-acre mark. And with 10,000 miles of shoreline, an extent greater than that of the Great Lakes, these new "Great Lakes of the South" are already being used by the public more intensively than the national parks.

From the beginning, the greatest controversy over the TVA has concerned its production of power—82.1 billion kilowatt-hours in 1967. On the one hand, there has been the obvious need of the valley people for electrification and their obvious enthusiasm for its results. ("The women went around turning the switches on and off," recalled one observer. "The light and wonder in their eyes was brighter than that from the lamps.") Through rural electric cooperatives and electrification loans, the TVA helped initiate the great power revolution on American farms that was carried on more widely in later years by the Rural Electrification Administration.

On the other hand, private power companies have contended that TVA has threatened their very existence. No answer has been found to abolish their fears or to displace their hopes that the Authority might some day be taken from public ownership and put into private hands. In defense of the TVA, one of its directors, Frank E. Smith, a former Mississippi Congressman, has made this statement: "The 800 square miles served by TVA get the most efficient power service in the country. Retail rates are the lowest in the nation, except for some parts of the hydro-rich Columbia valley. TVA and its distributors pay local and state tax equivalent to the average payments of private power systems. . . . [And] TVA competition does not seem to trouble the power companies which operate adjacent to TVA. They rank among the most efficient and most profitable private power systems in the country, with relatively low rates. Perhaps their proximity to TVA and their successful operation are no coincidence."

Taken as a whole, the history of the TVA has some important lessons for those who seek a balance of power between a strong federal government and effective local organizations. Between centralization and anarchy there lies the middle way of a regional approach to the problems and challenges of both natural and human resources. TVA is a functioning example by which men can measure the possibilities or drawbacks of such an approach.

And as long as the TVA exists, there will be controversy over it. One hazard now facing the public as well as the personnel of the agency itself is that the Authority may be considered a "success." Any pronouncement which would harden into a final evaluation betrays the nature of the Authority. It is not a monument to past vision so much as a reminder of future needs. It is a flexible, dynamic tool of democracy with battles to be fought and won.

For example, a new breed of TVA critics argue that in its lateness and laxness in facing up to the destructiveness of strip mining in the region (TVA's purchase of coal for its steam plants has provided the strip miners one of their largest markets) the Authority has not fulfilled its own purposes or the people's welfare.

There is irony, certainly, in the fact that in a traditionally independent region at the heart of the Border States, where people have been historically antagonistic to public planning, the most comprehensive, intensive and successful regional undertaking has become established as a worldwide inspiration. Perhaps the pragmatic attitude of some of those from outside the region who opposed TVA was reflected in the statement of one industrialist who built a large plant in the valley: "I don't believe in it. But as long as it's here I'm going to use it."

TVA: giant of the rivers

The great dam and gleaming electrical insulators in the picture at left tell the story of the double-barreled success of the Tennessee Valley Authority. The dam is one of 34 in a system that has converted the flood-prone Tennessee River into a series of spacious reservoirs called the "Great Lakes of the South." The insulators are part of the hydroelectric power system that helps TVA provide 18 million kilowatts—twice the power available to all New England—to some six million users in seven states.

But dams and electricity are only part of TVA's effort to develop the potential of the poor and long-neglected Tennessee Valley. TVA plants forests, teaches new farming techniques, and promotes community planning as part of a broad program to unite river, land and people for the benefit of all.

Giant insulators at a hydroelectric power plant rise against the backdrop of TVA's Fontana Dam. The dam, situated on the Little Tennessee River in North Carolina, produces 202,500 kilowatts of electric power.

Yesterday's torrents and trickles

The Tennessee River was 650 miles of sheer cussedness before TVA came along. During the spring, melting snows and heavy rains gorged the river until it overflowed its shallow channel, often inundating valley farms and low-lying cities like Chattanooga *(top left)*. In late summer, farms dried up and navigation came to a halt because the level of the river dropped so low that a man sometimes could wade across it at Knoxville *(below)*. It was primarily to halt this disastrous torrent-and-trickle cycle that the TVA came into being in 1933. By 1945 nine TVA dams on the Tennessee had turned the once-cantankerous river into a slow-flowing watery stairway whose "steps" gently lowered the river 515 feet from its headwater at Knoxville to its mouth near Paducah, Kentucky, where it joins the Ohio River. Boats and barges now go up and down the length of the river in all seasons, and the great floods of the past are fading memories. In 1957, when Chattanooga was threatened with one of the worst floods in its history, TVA technicians lowered the flood crest 22 feet by diverting water into upstream reservoirs—a move that saved 8,000 city acres from an estimated $66 million in flood damage.

Two views of Chattanooga, Tennessee *(left)*, photographed a century apart from Lookout Mountain, show the Tennessee River at its worst and best. The photo at the top was taken during the great flood of March 1867, when the river crested at a record 57.9 feet and most of the city lay under 30 feet of water. (A steamboat actually sailed down Chattanooga's main street.) Today, with floods controlled by TVA dams, the city flourishes beside a scenic, but subdued, river *(bottom)*.

Before the construction of Fort Loudon Dam by TVA in 1943, the Tennessee River at Knoxville, Tennessee, was often reduced to an 18-inch trickle at low water *(top right)*, making navigation impossible. Now, however, an 11-foot channel is maintained by means of carefully timed releases of water into Loudon's reservoir from tributaries upstream. Even heavily laden gasoline barges *(right)* can travel the entire length of the Tennessee to reach Knoxville at any time of year.

An empire of dams and power plants

The mighty imprint of TVA is indelibly stamped on the 40,000-square-mile watershed of the Tennessee River, shown in darker color below and shown in relationship to the rest of the United States at right. Within the watershed, 34 dams controlled by TVA—including six owned by ALCOA, the Aluminum Corporation of America—regulate the flow of the Tennessee and its tributaries, while permitting navigation as far as Knoxville. Flood-control reservoirs behind the dams can hold enough water to cover the state of Illinois up to a depth of eight inches. These reservoirs also serve as recreational areas; the largest of them, shaded in green, is the Land Between the Lakes, a 170,000-acre park bordered by the reservoirs of TVA's Kentucky Dam and the U.S. Army Corps of Engineers' Barkley Dam on the Cumberland River. As important as its dams are TVA's huge coal-burning and nuclear power plants. These plants now produce most of the 84 billion kilowatt-hours of electricity used annually by TVA's customers, more than the amount used by the entire nation of Italy.

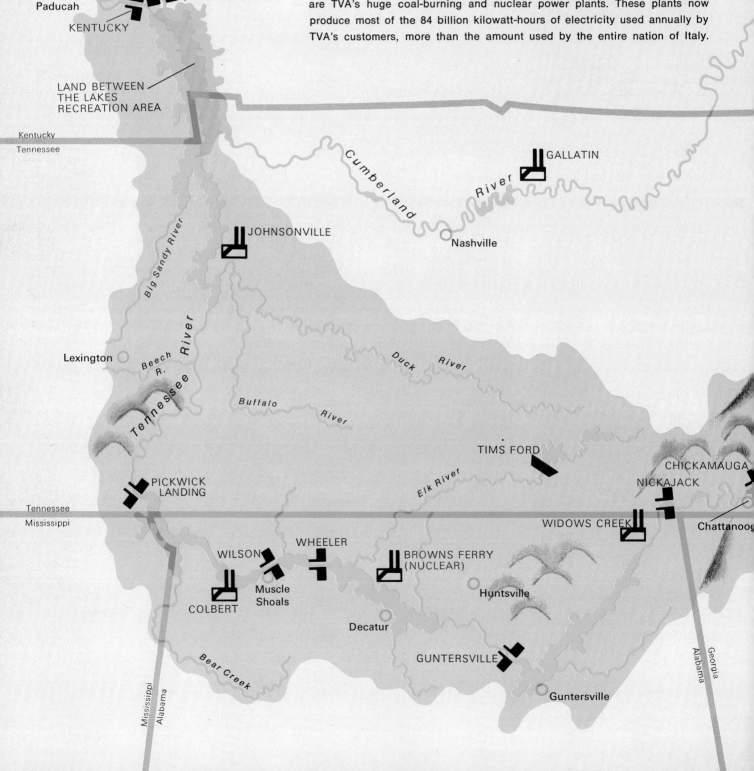

Ohio River

SHAWNEE

Paducah

BARKLEY
(U.S. CORPS)
(OF ENGINEERS)

KENTUCKY

LAND BETWEEN
THE LAKES
RECREATION AREA

Kentucky
Tennessee

Cumberland River

GALLATIN

Nashville

JOHNSONVILLE

Big Sandy River

Beech R.

Lexington

Tennessee River

Buffalo River

Duck River

TIMS FORD

PICKWICK
LANDING

Elk River

CHICKAMAUGA

NICKAJACK

Tennessee
Mississippi

WIDOWS CREEK

Chattanooga

WILSON

WHEELER

BROWNS FERRY
(NUCLEAR)

Huntsville

Muscle
Shoals

COLBERT

Decatur

Bear Creek

GUNTERSVILLE

Guntersville

Mississippi
Alabama

Georgia
Alabama

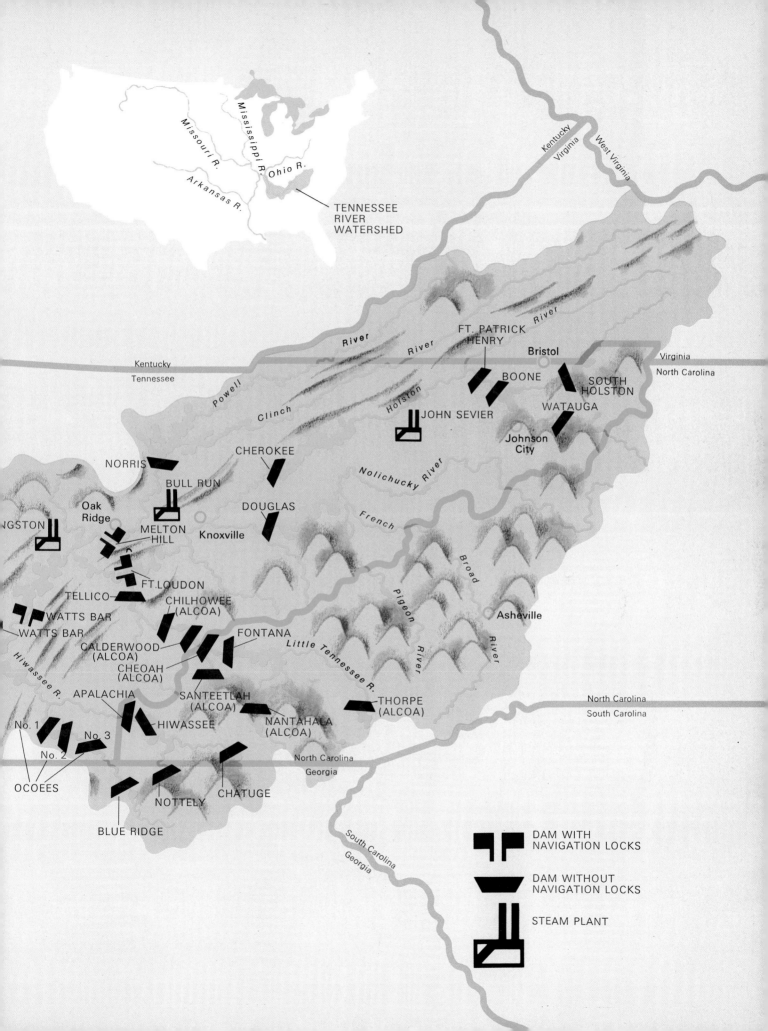

TENNESSEE
RIVER
WATERSHED

Mississippi R.

Missouri R.

Ohio R.

Arkansas R.

Kentucky
Virginia
West Virginia

Kentucky
Tennessee

Virginia
North Carolina

River

River

River

FT. PATRICK
HENRY

Bristol

BOONE

SOUTH
HOLSTON

JOHN SEVIER

WATAUGA

Powell

Clinch

Holston

Johnson
City

NORRIS

CHEROKEE

Nolichucky River

BULL RUN

French

Oak
Ridge

MELTON
HILL

DOUGLAS

Knoxville

NGSTON

Broad

FT.LOUDON

Pigeon

Asheville

TELLICO

CHILHOWEE
(ALCOA)

River

River

WATTS BAR

CALDERWOOD
(ALCOA)

FONTANA

Little Tennessee R.

WATTS BAR

CHEOAH
(ALCOA)

Hiwassee R.

APALACHIA

SANTEETLAH
(ALCOA)

THORPE
(ALCOA)

North Carolina
South Carolina

No. 1

HIWASSEE

NANTAHALA
(ALCOA)

No. 3

No. 2

North Carolina
Georgia

OCOEES

CHATUGE

NOTTELY

South Carolina

BLUE RIDGE

Georgia

DAM WITH
NAVIGATION LOCKS

DAM WITHOUT
NAVIGATION LOCKS

STEAM PLANT

New life for an ailing town

The town of Lexington, seen in the aerial photograph below, looks like many another rural county seat in western Tennessee. But, like its namesake in Massachusetts, it is a town that has been involved in a revolution. Tennessee's Lexington and the Beech River Valley make up one of 16 areas—all of them handicapped by devastated or unexploited resources—that TVA has singled out for special attention. In the Lexington-Beech River area, as shown on these pages, TVA has mounted a many-pronged attack upon basic economic problems in cooperation with local organizations and state agencies.

As recently as 1950, Lexington was being strangled by the economic depression that has persisted in the Tennessee Valley since the Civil War. Dependent on an agricultural economy, the town was losing population as thousands of acres of valley farmland eroded into worthless sand and unemployment soared. The per capita income of its residents was about $600, less than half the national average.

1. Beech Lake, a 900-acre reservoir, was planned by TVA to serve a number of different roles. An important unit in the Beech Valley flood-control system, the lake is the source of Lexington's water supply and its most promising area for residential growth. It has also become a popular recreational center. Stocked with bass, and enhanced by new access roads, parking facilities, a boat-launching platform and a beach, the lake is visited by some 70,000 people each summer.

2. A new water filtration plant, completed by TVA in 1967, broke the biggest bottleneck in the way of Lexington's development: an obsolete water system, barely able to meet the town's needs of a half million gallons of water a day. The new plant can process up to two million gallons of water a day from Beech Lake, and can be expanded to provide as much as five million gallons—an amount that probably will not be needed until well into the 21st Century.

3. The Hardin Screw Company is typical of a number of small industrial firms that have altered Lexington's economy by raising the number of manufacturing jobs in the area from 719 in 1950 to 3,890 in 1965. Aided by TVA surveys indicating the types of industry that could prosper in the area, the town has attracted companies that make brake bands and car doors, a wood-processing plant, a plywood manufacturer and a firm that processes local sand for industrial use. Two new industrial parks have been set aside for future development.

4. Eastern Shores, a TVA-planned subdivision, is a new residential area being planned on Beech Lake. Designed with an eye toward Lexington's anticipated population growth, its basic plan includes well-built homes, designed for use as year-round dwellings and served by paved access roads, underground electric lines, street lights and an up-to-date sewer system. These improvements are designed to provide Lexington with an additional inducement for new industry: excellent housing for executives at a location that is both convenient and scenic.

In less than two decades of intensive development under the guidance of TVA, Lexington and the Beech Valley have come a long way toward prosperity. The town's population has risen to almost 5,000, a jump of about 20 per cent; per capita income has more than doubled. New industries, providing almost 4,000 jobs, have reversed the flow of emigration, and the area's unemployment rate, which was double that of the nation as a whole, has been cut to half the national rate. Erosion has been checked by flood-control and reforestation programs, and farmers are applying newly learned lessons of scientific agriculture to their remaining acres.

Of TVA's many contributions, the most important has been the creation of Beech Lake behind the largest of eight new flood-control dams in the valley. The lake area provides Lexington's water supply, its recreational area and the site of its future residential growth—a combination of features that symbolize what TVA is trying to accomplish: to help make Lexington and its valley a good place to work and live.

5. Henderson County Courthouse in Lexington, a new building planned for the administrative needs of the area, is headquarters of the Beech River Watershed Development Authority, through which TVA and other outside help is channeled. The BRWDA sponsors programs to teach residents new industrial skills and will soon take part in TVA's unique "town lift" program. As part of this program, TVA experts will make an exhaustive survey of the town and suggest low-cost improvements—ranging from such essentials as wider roads and bigger parking lots to amenities like a unified color scheme for store fronts.

6A, 6B. New forests and pastureland indicate the success of TVA's extensive erosion-control program in the Beech Valley. For years, floods and heavy rains ate away the sandy soil, leaving wide areas of land too eroded for farming. Now some 18,500 acres of worthless land have been planted in pine trees (**6A**) providing the basis of a pulpwood and lumber industry in Lexington. Less eroded acres, planted with grass (**6B**), are now profitably used for cattle raising.

7. A demonstration farm, one of 49 so designated in 1967, shows local farmers how to use such modern techniques as fertilization and irrigation. A cooperative effort of TVA and the University of Tennessee, the demonstration farms have produced an average yield of 107 bushels of corn per acre—more than double the valley average. The demonstrators hope to raise this figure to 200 bushels with more improved techniques.

8. A TVA "rapid adjustment" farm offers an especially intensive demonstration of scientific agriculture. It surpasses the usual demonstration farm by showing the farmer how to attain maximum income from his acreage with a saturation program of such techniques as the computerized planning of farming schedules. For example corn farmers are encouraged to use a substantial part of their crop as feed for hogs rather than selling it; one such farmer was able to increase his total farm profit from $2,300 in 1962 to $16,500 three years later.

A little TVA on the Little Tennessee

"The work of TVA will never be over," said President John F. Kennedy in 1963 in a speech delivered on TVA's 30th anniversary. "There will always be new frontiers for it to conquer." One of these new frontiers runs along the tributaries of the Tennessee River, where the same kind of carefully planned effort that went into developing the potential of the Tennessee Valley is now being applied on a smaller scale in the valleys of the feeder streams. The $50 million Tellico Dam, shown at right being built across the mouth of the Little Tennessee River, was planned to add no electricity and little additional flood control to the existing TVA systems. Its principal purpose is the transformation of a rural vista *(below)* into Tellico Lake, an attractive industrial and recreational site accessible to highway, railroad and Tennessee River traffic. In drawing industry, vacationers and permanent residents to economically depressed eastern Tennessee, TVA is once more demonstrating its time-proved techniques for combining river, land and people in a common cause.

How a dam changes land uses is indicated on this photograph, a view of the Little Tennessee before completion of Tellico Dam.

Workers atop a completed section of Tellico Dam watch the construction of new forms for concrete.

6

The Beleaguered Mountaineer

He is a person of prickly pride—of an individualism so deeply ingrained that he may quit his first job in a factory if his foreman "orders him around like a dirty dog" rather than "asking him like a man." Yet he survives in part as a dependent receiving payments from welfare funds that cost taxpayers more than $14 million a month.

His homeland is one of the most scenic regions of America, where nature has been lavish with both beauty and resources. There are blue mountain ranges and green valleys; abundant water in broad rivers and flashing streams; a climate partaking of both the Deep South and the North, but never as extreme as either; a land of delicate fern and moss and lichen co-existing with rough "hells" of impenetrable rhododendron and tangled undergrowth and with barren outcroppings of rock ledges. Yet, in this handsome domain, his dwelling is often ugly and inadequate; his wastes—in slag heaps, polluted rivers and random litter—blight the land; his death rate from tuberculosis, a disease closely related to poor housing and diet, is 50

per cent higher than that of his fellow citizens in other parts of the country.

He is accustomed to long silences, he is considered laconic and uncommunicative, and on verbal achievement tests he scores below the national norm. Yet he shapes language with a vigor born of the oral tradition. For generations, history and folklore and hints for survival in his hard country were passed on by the spoken word—the word shared beside a fireplace on lonely winter nights, along woods trails or corn rows during long summer days, through periods of drawn-out waiting for birth or death. Thus, he uses strong antique words—"gaum" (to make messy), "beasties" and "waspies" (plural of beast and wasp)—with familiarity and relish. He may transform nouns into verbs: "I raised corn enough to *bread* me through the winter"; "It *pleasures* me to see the first catbird of spring." He may make a verb from an adjective: "Don't *contrary* me; I'm bulldog stubborn." He may use double nouns: "tooth-dentist," "widow-woman." He brings the humor, foibles and poetry of life into his place names: Cut-Shin, Hell-Fer-Sartain, Sandy Mush and Troublesome creeks; Craggy, Grandfather, Charlie's Bunion and Chunky Gal mountains; communities of Vixen, Viper, Trust and Luck. And if he cannot

Armed with an antique flintlock rifle, a mountain man poses warily before his crudely built cabin deep in the Appalachian Highlands. After generations of isolation in the hills, the mountaineers often take a suspicious view of strangers.

find the words to communicate with his hustling, half-deaf compatriots in the rest of America, perhaps it is because, as he might say, "I don't *confidence* them much."

He has experienced an isolation almost unparalleled in this country's history and from it flowed most of the special strengths and weaknesses he exhibits today. Yet now he is suddenly bound to the rest of the world—by television. Neither roads, schools, newspapers, radio nor the Sears, Roebuck catalogue shattered the barriers as completely as the TV aerials sprouting from every dwelling in his area. Spanking new brick split-level or crumbling log cabin, spacious white farmhouse or abandoned school bus turned into a temporary shelter —each thrusts up metal fingers to grasp words and pictures of the great wide world and transmit them to the little screen in the room below.

He is a rural, highly personal individual emerging into a complex industrialized, impersonal world—a world in which a family circle rarely extends beyond the immediate circle of parents and children. Yet, in the coal industry of his region, the first major unemployment crisis of the era of automation has erupted with calamitous effects, and the people least equipped to cope with such an upheaval are now expected to meet problems that, to a large extent, the rest of the country knows only academically.

He is poor, proud, cantankerous and of immense worth. He is his region's most important export and its most valuable resource. He is the mountaineer of the Southern Appalachians, which reach their grandest heights and darkest depths in the Border States.

According to one view of the region, Southern Appalachia is "the place where the axle broke"— and discouraged pioneers, too shiftless to mend the wagon, unpacked their meager belongings and settled down in the backwash of civilization to become picturesque, impoverished hillbillies. According to another view, Southern Appalachia is the place where a dream was realized—and free-spirited people who remembered the cloud-drenched highlands of Scotland and northern Ireland found a land to their liking and settled down in the vanguard of civilization to become mute, forgotten mountaineers. Each reading of the past —the accident of an axle or the fulfillment of a dream—is a half-truth. And it is by half-truths that most of America sees the contradictory people who live at the heart of the Border States.

In the mountains that run like a high ridge-pole across most of West Virginia, a slice of southwestern Virginia, eastern Kentucky, western North Carolina and eastern Tennessee, there settled representatives of many groups—the Tidewater English, the Cape Fear Scotch, the Pennsylvania Dutch and, above all others, the ubiquitous Scotch-Irish. But the famous "isolation" that these settlers found did not last very long. Through successive generations the mountaineer's lands, woods, waters, minerals and muscles were exploited by some of the largest corporations in America, and the exploiters often considered themselves the mountain man's superiors because they were shrewder in the labyrinths of the law and more attuned to America's manufacturing expansion. Others came, too: the word-peddlers— journalists, analysts, pollsters—who invaded the mountaineer's privacy and considered themselves his superiors because they were more articulate and more adept in adjusting to a standardized, industrialized way of life. Each exploitation left scars—on the landscape, the people, the national conscience. Now the scars can be healed only by genuine understanding and a reappraisal of human values.

It is well, for instance, to remember that this is an old land. Its ancient hills have been shaped through geologic ages by the abrasions of wind and water, freeze and thaw, and its long-enduring people have been molded by generations of living in a harsh (yet magnificent) landscape. Between the mountaineers and their land there exists a personal and paradoxical relationship. They can destroy it almost casually, yet cling to it ardently. They know that the natural world is filled with mystery and wonder, as well as nourishment and hardship, and they may still plant crops by certain signs of the moon, consider themselves forewarned of impending disasters by the calls of certain night birds and use herbs to cure a variety of ills.

Not all of these activities can be considered purely local in scope and influence, either. The herbs of these mountains, for example, play an important part in American medicine. From western North Carolina alone come 30 per cent of all the crude botanicals produced in the United States; the Border States as a whole contain a greater variety of these botanicals than any other region in the nation. There are families of herb hunters who supplement their farm income or make the bulk of their cash livelihood by ranging the forests and fields for roots, berries, bark and leaves to supply drug manufacturers. From the time they are children these gatherers are taught to identify a large number of plants and shrubs and to distinguish the useful from the useless, the medicinal from the poisonous.

They search for calamus root and wild cherry bark and goldenseal and bloodroot, the leaves of witch hazel, pokeberries, slippery elm bark, sassafras and dozens more. After they gather the plants, they must clean and dry them with great care. And not until their bright leaves and pungent roots are almost ready for the wholesaler do they know exactly how much they will bring, for crude drugs are one of the few items still directly priced on the open market by immediate supply and demand.

If nature provided leaves and roots for healing, mountain people have also believed that it provided a rhythm by which life might be measured. Their chronicles have not involved punch-clocks or organized schedules; instead, time has been remembered by a season's turning. "It was dogwood winter when my boy came home." "She had her baby during the last full moon." "I always sun my quilts during corn planting."

Professor Marion Pearsall of the University of Kentucky has explained this special relationship between the mountaineer and his place as a major point of difference "between the Southern Appalachians and the rest of the country. Thornton Wilder once commented that Americans are 'abstract.' By that he meant that we are oriented to everywhere and everything, a fact that makes both geographic and social mobility fairly painless for those who are unencumbered by strong ties to places or things. But in Southern Appalachia it is the concreteness of life that is valued, the particular locations and the particular possessions."

Life is not easy in the mountains, but people may find their own unique satisfactions in living there. Many have found a deeply satisfying style of life. In a plea for understanding, one of them voiced the deep inarticulate frustrations of a multitude when he said to a visitor: "Bring us your northern culture, but leave us our civilization."

Unfortunately, most visitors have responded not with understanding, but with stereotyped interpretations. And of all the stereotypes that afflict America's understanding of itself—the tight-fisted Yankee, the inert Indian, the irresponsible Negro —none is more steadfast or devastating or more paradoxical than that of the comical Southern mountaineer. On the one hand he is a slack-jawed, rifle-toting, moonshining cartoonist's buffoon whose chief occupation is evading the revenuers, beget-

ting children and collecting welfare. On the other hand he is a stalwart, dulcimer-plucking, sentimentalist's legend whose chief pastime is speaking a quaint Elizabethan dialect, whittling out the toys he calls play pretties and defending his tender honor. Each stereotype persists, with the tragic result that the mountaineer seems set apart from the mainstream of American experience.

Many descriptions of the mountain people have helped to create these stereotypes. There were the reports of William Byrd, for example, which set the pattern early. In 1728 Byrd left his elegant Tidewater home, Westover, to help lay out a dividing line between Virginia and North Carolina, and ever since he recorded his opinions of the country beyond the Tidewater, North Carolina backwoodsmen have expected the worst from their haughty neighbors. Byrd described North Carolina as a land where "the Men, for their Parts, just like the Indians, impose all the Work upon the poor Women. They make their Wives rise out of their Beds early in the Morning, at the same time that they lye and Snore, till the Sun has run one third of his course, and disperst all the unwholesome Damps. Then, after Stretching and Yawning for half an Hour, they light their Pipes, and, under the Protection of a cloud of Smoak, venture out into the open Air; tho', if it happens to be never so little cold, they quickly return Shivering into the Chimney corner. When the weather is mild, they stand leaning with both their arms upon the corn-field fence, and gravely consider whether they had best go and take a Small Heat at the Hough [hoe]: but generally find reasons to put it off till another time."

In 1941, more than two centuries later, that genteel Southern chronicler, William Alexander Percy of Mississippi, exhibited the same unfamiliarity that breeds contempt. Looking up from his Delta plantation to the hill country, Percy wrote that the mountain whites were probably the most unprepossessing breed of men on the face of the earth. "I can forgive them as the Lord God forgives, but admire them, trust them, love them— never. Intellectually and spiritually they are inferior to the Negro, whom they hate." (If any despised hillbillies had read this passage, they might have felt that if the Lord God dispensed judgment as carelessly as the archangel Percy, forgiveness was beside the point.)

The ultimate in gloom was achieved, however, by the historian Arnold Toynbee, who concluded that the Appalachian mountain people are "no better than barbarians. They have relapsed into illiteracy and witchcraft. . . . They are the American counterparts of the latter-day white barbarians of the Old World—Rifis, Albanians, Kurds, Pathans, and Hairy Ainus."

In response, Rupert Vance of the University of North Carolina struck a note between despair and comedy by describing his people as including three kinds of folk: "The Lord's poor, destitute by misfortune; the devil's poor, stranded by their own follies; and poor devils from worthless stock who never were nor could be otherwise."

In a more positive vein, Tennessee historian John Trotwood Moore characterized the Scotch-Irish highlanders of his state in this way: "If abused, they fight; if their rights are infringed, they rebel; if forced, they strike; and if their liberties are threatened, they murder. . . . They eat meat and their bread is always hot."

In 1962 Justice William O. Douglas visited the Cades Cove area of the Great Smoky Mountains National Park. Through long conversations with the natives of this mountain-rimmed expanse of woods and meadow Douglas learned much about the past and present of the mountains. He remembered families he met as "the kindest, most thoughtful, most generous people I have known. At the same time they were the proudest and the most independent. I found in Cades Cove the warm heart and the bright conscience of America."

What is the stranger to believe? He can find facts and statistics in plenty: about 95 per cent of the Southern Appalachian people are white, 99 per cent of them are native-born, and more Southern Appalachian workers are now gainfully employed in manufacturing than in farming and mining combined. But are these mountain people Toynbee's "Hairy Ainus" or Douglas' "bright conscience"? Are they victims or heroes? Perhaps an incident that occurred in a county courtroom will serve as indirect reply. A lawyer was trying to get a reluctant witness to testify as to the character of the defendant. After the witness geed and hawed a while, the lawyer pinned him down sharply: "Just tell us, sir, does this defendant have a good character or a bad?" The old man answered: "Now I'll tell you, it's just a little of both."

One fact is essential to an understanding of the mountain region: there are at least two distinct Appalachias and therefore at least two distinct kinds of mountain men. One Appalachia consists essentially of the coal-mining country; the other is made up of the rest of the mountain country.

The coal area is rural, yet it is also one of the most highly specialized and industrialized pockets in the nation. Most of its counties are in eastern Kentucky and West Virginia, with a few clustered in western Virginia, western Kentucky and eastern Tennessee counties. This area has experienced economic crises, labor strife and bloodshed and—most recently—automation and joblessness.

Understandably, the people of this coal region differ in many ways from their fellow mountaineers. They live in what is probably the roughest terrain of the Southern mountains. Their housing is the poorest in Appalachia. They suffered brutal experiences during the unionizing of the mines—struggles against the use of convict labor in Briceville, Tennessee; bloody marches and savage encounters in Mingo County, West Virginia; and in Harlan County, Kentucky, to name only three of the better-known battlefields of the coal wars. They have known the bitterness of "boom and bust"—in the quick rise and crumbling disintegration of coal villages, in depressions that strangled whole communities in a sudden convulsion. Most recently, they have been confronted with a new form of destruction: strip mining. The rapid rise of this method for gouging out the rich coal seams is rendering much of the mountain man's labor unnecessary and much of his land uninhabitable.

Strip mining is precisely what its name suggests. Mammoth scraping and boring machines (some of them as high as 20-story buildings) and powerful explosives tear away the topsoil. When a seam of coal is exposed, it may be traced by a single cut along the contours of a ridge, or a whole mountaintop may be scalped. After the machines and explosives have done their job, the refuse (trees, plants, mulch and forest-cover) is pushed down the mountainsides, while huge power shovels scoop up the exposed coal and load it into trucks. In an underground mine it would take many times the number of men and hours used in this operation to dig out the same amount of coal. As of the spring of 1967 strip mining was yielding one third of the area's coal production, but it accounted for only 18 per cent of the coal-mine labor force.

The coal country of Appalachia is becoming a blighted area whose landscape resembles the barren, blasted surface of the moon. As the green cover of the steep hills has been scraped away and overturned into the narrow valleys, roads and houses and streams have been engulfed. The raw dirt left behind after the coal is extracted is a thick sludge of mud in rainy weather and a choking bed of dust in drought. From one mountain slope to the next, the cuts run wide and deep and the wreckage accumulates.

Kentucky lawyer and author Harry M. Caudill, a controversial spokesman against indiscriminate strip mining, has argued for a tax that would leave a portion of the money made from a mine in the county where it is located. In his *Night Comes to the Cumberlands,* published in 1963, he focused national attention on the problem. "Coal," he said, "has always cursed the land in which it lies. When men begin to wrest it from the earth it leaves a legacy of foul streams, hideous slag heaps and polluted air. . . . It mars but never beautifies. It corrupts but never purifies."

In February 1968, when a Senate subcommittee on Employment, Manpower and Poverty headed by Senator Robert Kennedy met for a hearing in Neon, Kentucky, Caudill appeared as a witness in the town's chilly, barnlike, dilapidated gymnasium. With the fervor and oratory of a mountain evangelist, he made a powerful statement: "In the last decades of the 19th Century and the first few years of the 20th Century . . . speculators came into the hills. . . . For prices ranging from 10 cents up to $5.00 per acre they bought all the underlying minerals and mineral substances, together with the right to extract them. Practically everybody sold. Today, in Letcher County, a typical Appalachian county, the minerals under 94 per cent of the land are owned by seven or eight companies, each of which is chartered in another state."

Caudill went on to say, "Today the poorest people and the most prosperous corporations in the United States are found right here in eastern Kentucky. Of the 30 poorest counties in America, 20 of them are in eastern Kentucky. . . . In some counties more than 25 per cent of the people are on public assistance. In the southern coal fields some 70,000 men are totally disabled as a result of silicosis and pneumoconiosis [lung diseases due to the inhalation of dust particles]."

Many of the weatherbeaten people who packed the gymnasium could have testified to the truth of what Caudill had said. Some of them did not know the other facts he had marshalled: "While the mountains are teeming with poor and underprivileged people, they also bristle with some of the biggest and most prosperous names in America. Within 30 miles of where we sit today there are operations owned by subsidiaries of Ford Motor Company, International Harvester, United States Steel Corporation, Bethlehem Steel Corporation and Republic Steel Corporation. . . . Little of the great wealth generated here in these hills remains behind. Tens of millions of dollars worth of coal was marshalled here in the yards at Neon and sent to the markets of the world during the years when Letcher County school teachers were fortunate to earn $75 a month."

Caudill proposed specific programs to improve the situation, most notably a federal tax on mining profits to help the counties break their cycle of poverty with improved education, health facilities and public services. But the main thrust of his remarks was directed to all Americans. He showed that the dilemmas of the coal area of Appalachia were due less to the short-sightedness or inadequacies of a group of comic-strip caricatures than to the myopic and selfish operations of persons outside the Border States.

The second Appalachia has its problems, too—none of them quite so severe as those afflicting the coal area, but thorny enough to challenge the best of local and national leadership. The mountain areas of the Border States need a more balanced use of their resources; they need a fuller and more diversified industrialization; and they need development of the educational, social and cultural benefits that flow from an adequate economy. As a major step in creating such an economy, they need to make their region more accessible and attractive to tourists—and in this big job, according to a recent report, "the expensive things are being done, but not the difficult inexpensive ones." For this job, and for all the others, the second Appalachia must produce new, resourceful leaders.

If Harry Caudill speaks for the beleaguered mountaineers of the coal country, an earlier writer, Horace Kephart, was the voice of all those other hill people, especially the North Carolinians and Tennesseans of the Great Smokies area.

Kephart was a librarian in St. Louis when, one day in 1904, he abandoned the book stacks, his wife and their six children and—like Gauguin embarking for the South Seas—sought out a primitive and luxuriant region where he might lose himself. When he tried to learn something about the mountains of North Carolina before leaving the Midwest, he could find not even "a magazine article, written within this generation, that described the land and its people." He later said, "Had I been going to Teneriffe or Timbuctu, the libraries would have furnished information a-plenty; but about this housetop of eastern America they were strangely silent."

Pale and in poor health when he arrived in the mountains, Horace Kephart spent the rest of his life gaining an intimate knowledge of the natural world and the people around him. During these years he regained his health and became an authority on camping and woodcraft. What was more important, he worked to preserve the wilderness domain, he helped to create the Great Smoky Mountains National Park and he wrote a book, *Our Southern Highlanders,* which has remained a classic in its field since its publication in 1913.

With the perspective of a well-read outsider, Kephart looked clearly and closely at the mountain people and every aspect of their lives. He became the friend and advocate of these people, who had been "beleaguered by nature," and "ghettoed in the midst of a civilization that is as aloof from them as if it existed . . . on another planet." Moonshiners, farmers, hunters, feuders, young and old —all of them accepted and befriended the outlander. And for his part, Kephart accepted them all, accepted the crudeness and grace of their lives, the codes and values of their society. They were, he insisted, a "people of keen intelligence and strong initiative when they can see anything to win." But Horace Kephart's final words on his highlanders are as true today as they were half a century ago: "Slash, crash, go the devastating forces of progress. The great need of our mountaineers to-day is trained leaders of their own. The future of Appalachia lies mostly in the hands of those resolute native boys and girls who win the education fitting them for such leadership."

Fifty years later another book made a similar and even more somber plea. When *The Southern Appalachian Region: A Survey,* initiated and directed by W. D. Weatherford and financed by the Ford Foundation, was published in 1962, it reemphasized the need for leadership. But it also pointed out: "The amount of money spent for educating a Southern Appalachian pupil in 1958 was only one-half of the national average. . . . The regional handicaps are not being overcome, but rather are becoming more severe. The breach of inequality between the region and the nation becomes greater with the forward movement of our country. This is cause for national alarm."

During recent decades, new industries from other regions and tourists from all parts of the world have come in increasing numbers to the Southern mountains. Those who have sought to know the people there, through necessity or simple curiosity, have discovered that it is dangerous to describe any of their characteristics too glibly.

An example: the mountaineer's individualism. America was founded on the principle of each man's right to dignity, opportunity and freedom of choice. Yet the mountain man's precious independence can lead him to reject necessary advice. A Presbyterian minister with a parish in a West Virginia county concluded, in some desperation, "The mountaineer recognizes no experts." This independence may bring misunderstandings in an industrial plant. The personnel manager of a large factory in east Tennessee said of his mountain workers, "Everybody in this region has a little bit of red in his hair; you can work with them but you can't push them." And the same individualism may prevent the mountain man from cooperating in work where a sense of community is essential and individual labors must be coordinated in group efforts. The lack of strong community spirit is one of the most serious problems in Southern Appalachia today.

On the other hand, the mountaineer's individualism and awareness of personal dignity often produce the most exquisite courtesy. It is a courtesy compounded of pride, loyalty and a rare sense of privacy. In one of its more humorous manifestations it led one mountain man, himself a convicted felon who had served time in prison, to quit his job in an electronics plant because a foreman kept saying "damn" before the women workers.

At its best this courtesy can call forth glowing tributes from outsiders. In 1944, for example, the famous war correspondent Ernie Pyle was stationed in England with some boys from east Tennessee. This observer of men said, "It seems to me that these boys feel more at home over here than any of the other troops. . . . A few have been to college, but some of them cannot read or write. And yet I defy you to find more real gentlemen among our troops than in a camp of these so-called hillbillies. There is a simple genuineness about them that shows in every word they speak. They are courteous, friendly, and trusting—all by instinct."

Another aspect of the mountaineer's character and history has led to his reputation for violence. (One wit defined Appalachia as the territory "below the Smith and Wesson line.") The reputation is not undeserved. There have been feuds, coal and tobacco wars, and perennial killings over women, dogs and line fences. Harry Caudill takes

Strip mining, diagrammed at left, is a swift, economical—and destructive—method used to extract the layers of coal that lie within 100 feet of the surface throughout much of the Border States. The land is first cleared by a bulldozer *(upper left),* and the overburden—the layers of dirt and rock that cover the coal —is stripped away by a giant strip shovel (some shovels are as tall as a 20-story building and can lift more than 200 tons in a single bite). The waste material is stacked in a ridge-shaped "spoil bank," forming one side of a wide trench that has a floor of almost pure coal. A smaller "load shovel" digs out the coal and loads it into trucks. The trench is then buried beneath the new spoil bank from the next trench. The result is one of the depressing sights of Appalachia— a series of rocky ridges, resembling a gigantic washboard *(page 154).*

note of the statistics wrought by pistol, knife and whiskey. "At Pikeville," he says, writing of his native Kentucky, "an elderly attorney still maintains an office for the practice of law. In nearly sixty years at the bar he has defended more than a thousand mountaineers charged with 'willful murder.' A hundred miles away in 'bloody Harlan' the Commonwealth Attorney has preserved a record of the murder indictments he has prosecuted. As this is written, his list stands above six hundred. Each of these gentlemen can, almost certainly, claim a record which has never been equaled or surpassed in the world of English jurisprudence."

Dreadful as such violence is, it has another side. Mountaineers have helped bring the Border States a valiant record in war, for they have consistently produced more than their share of the fighting men. Tennessee, for example, has been called the "Volunteer State." East Tennessee mountaineers volunteered for the battles of King's Mountain in the Revolution and of Horseshoe Bend and New Orleans in the War of 1812; when President James K. Polk called for 50,000 men from all the nation in the Mexican War of 1846, Tennessee alone offered more than 30,000 volunteers (the state quota was 2,800) . An American folk hero of World War I was a middle-Tennessee mountain squirrel

hunter named Alvin C. York. On October 8, 1918, armed only with a pistol and a rifle, York killed 25 Germans, captured 132 more and put 35 machine guns out of action. In 1940 to 1941, according to journalist John Temple Graves, the national proportion of volunteer enlistment to draftee inductions was 49.8 per cent, while the proportion in Kentucky was 123.4 per cent.

Another aspect of the mountaineer's readiness to fight should also be held in mind. In *Stinking Creek,* a book about the life and people of one remote Kentucky valley, Louisville newspaperman John Fetterman observed, "On Stinking Creek there are no muggings, robberies, stabbings, rapes. Yet every boy carries a pocket knife—not as a weapon, but as a symbol of responsible manhood." What is extraordinary is the fact that these armed and violent people commit few crimes of malice or of greed. "On Stinking Creek you can leave your car unlocked with its load of cameras, typewriter, and personal belongings without fear. Where else can you do this?"

The final word may be left by a genteel but hard-headed lady named Mary Breckinridge, who founded a unique health service in eastern Kentucky's Leslie County. Originally designed to help mothers and infants, Miss Breckinridge's Frontier

Nursing Service later sent nurses on horseback to serve patients of all kinds throughout the mountains. In her autobiography, published in 1952, Miss Breckinridge said, "Our nurses go out on calls with any man, anywhere, at any hour of the night, if he comes for them. Our young couriers can ride alone over the most remote trails with a safety that would not be theirs in some parts of our great cities."

For better or worse, those "great cities" are getting to know the Southern Appalachian mountain people, for the region is now contributing to the expansion of some of our largest urban centers. Between 1950 and 1960 a net out-migration of more than a million people took place—a number equal to nearly one fifth of the region's total population in 1950. And during this decade, for the first time since settlers struggled over the tall ridges and straggled down the long valleys, Appalachia showed a loss of population. Even a high birth rate could not span the widening gulf between emigration and population growth.

One student of the region has remarked that there are now four Rs in mountain education: Reading, 'Riting, 'Rithmetic—and Route U.S. 25 North. And as more and more mountaineers have taken this route, which leads to Lexington, Kentucky, and points north, new problems have been created at both ends of the journey. Among the departing millions, the majority have been single persons and young families. They have been generally better educated than those they have left behind, but not as well educated as those among whom they have settled. In many urban areas the status of the Appalachian migrant, with his lack of technical skills, his unique social experience and cultural values, is an inferior one. Each of these facts means trouble—trouble for the mountaineer who leaves his native region and trouble for the community he goes to.

So the mountains, with their poverty and wealth, cut across the consciousness of the Border States — and all America. The mountain people have overcome many enemies, weathered many storms, endured many griefs. In a land of "make do or do without" they have made: furniture and pottery, carvings and homespun textiles, hand-forged ironware, musical instruments, brooms, toys, jewelry—the necessities and minor luxuries of creative people using what nature put in their way.

Industries that have moved into the Southern mountains have discovered that hands made strong and nimble by years of milking and farming and mending machinery are adept at assembling electronics parts and television sets, working at machines that turn out rayon and a variety of other synthetic fibers, and making everything from parachutes to bandages to high-fashion cashmere sweaters. People whose traditions included the necessity of canning each summer's surplus for the winter pantry now work in a baby-food cannery in western North Carolina and in the factory of Stokely-Van Camp, one of the largest food packers and canners in the United States, which had its beginnings in 1898 in Newport, Tennessee, in the shadow of the Great Smokies. A people who for generations have used the earth's materials to create beautiful and utilitarian objects are producing fine glassware in West Virginia. And hill people are providing the muscle and skill to turn the wheels of a giant aluminum plant, paper factories, a sprawling complex of chemical and fiber plants. Twentieth Century industry is bringing the rhythms—and incomes—of a new day to some corners of Appalachia.

In other corners of Southern Appalachia, mountain people are helping resort developments to mushroom in areas once called the "back of beyond." Taking advantage of high altitudes and steep slopes, ski runs now dominate dozens of mountainsides, with attendant chalets spattering a bright new architecture in the surrounding woods and hilltops and snug coves. Golf courses emerge in unsuspected valleys; rustic tourist lodges look out upon rugged scenic grandeur.

In these recreational developments, the tourist becomes a sort of mountaineer-by-adoption. And the central fact of the mountaineer's life—be he native or adopted, a farmer turning his rocky acres with a bull-tongue plow or a hiker tramping along the Appalachian Trail—is the magnificence of his surroundings. It is heritage and gift and responsibility. It is a tender fern frond unfolding in the mulch of fecund spring woods; it is summer afternoon shadows purpling the long ranges of the Blue Ridge and the Smokies; it is leaf-smoke and dry grass sweetening the hazy golden days of autumn. It is all of these—and every other smell, sight, sound, taste and touch, in a place where the senses can still find fulfillment.

A middle-aged mountain woman said it, after she had returned to the hills from a brief transplantation in Jersey City. "I wanted to get back where I could taste water and breathe air and keep touch with living things."

Furniture builder Shadrach Mace of North Carolina shapes
a part of a chair after the fashion of the pioneers. After
clamping a square length of wood in a drawhorse—a primitive
vise tightened by a pedal—he painstakingly forms the wood
into a round rung or leg with a two-handed knife.

Artisans of the Appalachians

The pioneers who worked their way down into the
back country of the Southern Appalachians could
carry little with them. Once settled, they made by hand
nearly everything they needed—furniture, tools, cloth,
even musical instruments and toys. To their tasks they
brought the skills of their European ancestors, applied
to the natural resources of a new land. They used
native walnut and hickory for making furniture, bark
for tanning leather, berries and herbs for dyeing wool,
and cotton and flax for spinning and weaving cloth.

With an intense pride of craftsmanship, the isolated
mountain people went on making things by hand long
after the rest of the country turned to machine-made
goods. In recent years, teachers and community
workers have encouraged many older people to revive
their skills and have found markets for handmade
chairs, playthings, homespun cloth, quilts and
musical instruments. Today mountain handicrafts
bring as much as $10 million a year to the region.

Photographs by Bruce Roberts

Sturdy chairs and delicate dulcimers

The highland forests provide a wood for nearly every purpose and mountain craftsmen take full advantage of the variety. Using tough woods like hickory, Shadrach Mace *(left)* makes chairs so strong that they usually outlive the people who buy them. Mace scorns the use of glue: his chairs hold together because he drives dry, well-aged rungs into green legs, which tighten around the rungs as they dry. Using woods such as maple or cherry, wood-carver Edd Presnell *(below)* shapes stringed instruments called dulcimers. The dulcimer, which is plucked with a goose quill or a sliver of hickory, has an uncertain origin, but has been popular in the highlands since the days of the pioneers. Its plaintive sound is a perfect accompaniment for the singing of old English ballads, which are a living part of the mountain heritage.

Edd Presnell cuts delicate sound holes in a dulcimer with an "extended hourglass" body. At left is a carved mahogany table top.

Standing in the doorway of his workshop, Shadrach Mace shows two products of his craft: a straight-backed chair and a rocker.

From yarns and dyes to "kiverlids"

Catherine Marony, a craftswoman at the Penland School of Crafts, feeds raw wool fibers onto a rotating spindle. Driven by a spinning wheel (not seen in picture), the spindle twists fibers into yarn.

Skeins of wool, hung to dry by Miss Marony outside the dyeing shed at the Penland School, glow with the warm rusts, browns and reds of natural dyes. The dried yarn will be ready for the weaving looms.

Rhododendron leaves are boiled to produce a natural gray-green. Plants native to the mountains provide all colors except blue; a blue dye is made by growing indigo, originally imported from India.

Almost forgotten by the early 1900s, the art of weaving cloth has been revived at a number of Appalachian schools. At North Carolina's Penland School of Crafts, for example, mountain people have been encouraged to make dyes from bark, berries, roots and leaves, to resurrect their old weaving patterns, or "drafts," and to set up their looms again. Many mountain craftsmen now turn out woolen coverlets (which they call kiverlids or kivers) from local materials. It is arduous work, and slow. When one mountain weaver received an order for 12 coverlets a month, she turned it down. "It would take we 'uns nigh one year or more afore we could have that many kivers wove," she explained. "We will have to raise more sheep, shear them, pick and wash the wool, card it and spin it, then collect the bark and such to color it. Then we will have to get the loom all set up, fix the warp and beam [secure] it, then get a draft, and thread the warp for the pattern we want, then tie the loom, and then we will be ready for weaving. . . . It's no child's play to make a kiver." Yet the work is worth the effort. The homespun coverlets surpass their machine-made counterparts and are prized by collectors in many parts of the country.

The finished product, a coverlet woven according to an old pattern, or "draft," lies on rocky ground. The edges are not sewn in a binding, but are left in strands to hang free as a fringe.

Playthings
from cornhusks

The original settlers of the Southern Appalachians did not waste even their "shucks"—the cast-off husks from corncobs. Like the mountain people of today, the pioneers grew corn as a staple food and an animal feed; there has never been a lack of husks to work with. The mountain craftsmen have used them as raw material for mats and rugs, collars for work animals, and picturesque children's dolls. The dolls on these pages were made by May Ritchie Deschamps, a member of a family of gifted North Carolina craftsmen and folk singers. Each doll is made entirely of corn shucks except for the hat (which is crocheted of raffia) and the hair (which is made of another waste product, corn silk). One of the best known of the mountain craft products, the delightful dolls have been sold as far away as India and Australia.

May Deschamps finishes a corn-shuck doll. Mrs. Deschamps' family is steeped in craft traditions; her mother still wove rugs at 89.

With her inked-on face and rosy cheeks, a pert doll looks like a pioneer woman standing against a background of North Carolinian woods.

Pottery from the mountain clay

Pottery making in the highlands dates from the 1700s, when settlers first dug into layers of clay just below the surface soil to make cooking pots and table dishes. At Ben Owen's pottery in Seagrove, North Carolina *(below)*, clay is still worked as in colonial days. It is dug nearby, shaped or "thrown" on a wheel powered by the potter's foot, and then fired in a simple wood-burning kiln. Owens and his assistant mastered the methods at the Jugtown Pottery, a famous traditional pottery near Steeds, North Carolina, where the old designs and techniques were preserved and taught. Other potters in the region use modern machines and methods, but they are not the only source of new designs. Even the traditional workers constantly experiment with different clays and glazes to create highly individual products.

Three utilitarian examples of Ben Owen's pottery exhibit the simple forms and warm earth colors that characterize his work. At right is a squat round teapot. Below it, a pair of sturdy candlesticks rests on a windowsill. In the bottom picture is a heavy lidded casserole dish designed for cooking baked beans or slow-simmering stews.

Bruce Yow, a craftsman at Owen's pottery, stokes the fire in the shop's kiln with lengths of pine. Only a few wood-burning kilns are still used in the mountains; most are now heated by gas or electricity.

With a patchwork cat at her feet, Mrs. Ward completes a patchwork quilt.

The intricacies of a patchwork quilt

In earlier days the mountain women made patchwork quilts to give their daughters when they "stepped off" to get married. Today the work brings in cash income (many an uneducated woman has quilted her boys through school). But the method of making quilts has never changed. They consist of three layers: the bottom a single piece of cloth, the middle a warm material like flannel, and the top a mosaic of bits of cloth pieced together in a colorful pattern. The layers are joined by cord "ties" or by delicate needle work called "quilting"—tiny stitches that make a pattern of their own.

Mrs. Jeff Ward of Bakersville, North Carolina, who made the quilts at right, uses traditional designs with names like Bear's Paw *(top row, right and left)*, Black Diamond *(top, middle)* and Skip Around the Mountain, shown in two variations in the bottom row. Some names stand for the appearance of the design—stylized bear footprints can be seen in Bear's Paw. Others derive from the way the quilt is made; in Skip Around the Mountain the quilter starts with five squares at the center and works irregularly outwards.

7

Voices of the Past and Present

In a rich literature and a distinctive music, the creative artists of the Border States have sought to identify and interpret their experience of the region. Rough-hewn or finely polished, with wit honed sharp as a whittler's knife and belly-laughter as strong as hides home-tanned to leather, they have conveyed this experience in fresh, specific terms that have enriched readers and audiences in the nation as a whole. Above all, whether entertainers or philosophers, they have been lively—sparked by a zest for life and its many contradictions, its astonishments, its possibilities.

The experience has not been a simple one. In literature particularly, the Border States have exhibited a sharp contrast between people living at the inland heart of the region and people living in the lowlands, open to the intercourse of rivers and ocean. There is, for example, no more startling antithesis in American literature than that between one of the earliest writers of the colonial Tidewater, William Byrd II, and one of the earliest writers of the backwoods, George W. Harris,

Dancers form a human totem pole in a scene from *The Lost Colony*, the "symphonic drama" by Paul Green that was first staged in Manteo, North Carolina, in 1937. Dealing with the Lost Colony of Roanoke, the pageant is presented every summer.

who won fame as the creator of Sut Lovingood. Each was an authentic voice of his region. Byrd's detailed diaries and records reflected the past in which Tidewater traditions and habits were rooted, the gentility and manners and attitudes of the Old World transplanted to new surroundings. Harris' boisterous tall tales, written more than a century later, were forerunners of the future, in which raw frontier jokes and pranks would be refined into a literature uniquely and vigorously American. To know these two writers is to know the full flavor of the region—sometimes as smooth as one of Byrd's bottles of Madeira, sometimes as full of kicks as Harris' home-brewed whiskey.

Byrd, called William the Great and the Pepys of the Old Dominion, was born in 1674 near the present city of Richmond. From his father he inherited 25,000 acres of land, high social and official position, and a shrewd practicality. On his own he acquired more than 150,000 additional acres, a cultivated mind and a library of more than 3,600 volumes, one of the largest collections in the American colonies. Though there were few facilities for publishing books in the Virginia of his time, Byrd wrote throughout his long life—primarily for his own satisfaction and the occasional amusement of his friends. And his life was a busy one. The renovation and expansion of his elegant Georgian mansion, Westover, helped to keep him in debt for years, and running its plantation called for energy, patience and judgment. He was a tobacco planter and merchant, a member of the House of Burgesses, collector of the royal revenues, and a diplomatic agent of the colony.

As an official observer at the survey of the dividing line between Virginia and North Carolina in 1728, he kept both a public record, *The History of the Dividing Line,* and a private one, *The Secret History of the Line.* The first was not published until nearly a century after his death; the second did not appear in print until 1929. Byrd's diaries, a daily account of his adult years, were kept in a system of personal shorthand that remained undeciphered until recent years. The publication of two segments of the diaries in 1941 and 1942 established him, belatedly but firmly, as one of America's leading colonial writers.

Perhaps the most impressive feature of these writings is the range of Byrd's interests. Again and again he writes of rising early so that he may read in Greek, Latin, Hebrew, French, Italian or Dutch before breakfast. His insatiable curiosity stimulated experiments in botany and medicine and explorations of the colonial back country. More than any of his illustrious compatriots, he provides intimate glimpses of daily life on one of the great plantations with its mundane details and responsibilities, its frequent pleasures and satisfactions.

No writer exemplifies better than Byrd the differences between the colonial people of the Border States and those of the Puritans' New England. In Byrd's Anglican devoutness there was no gloom and little doom. He saw no merit in abstraction in his writing or abstention in his personal life; he ate heartily, drank merrily, loved variously, prayed nightly, conversed urbanely, executed his business decisively, observed everything around him precisely—and set it all down in sparkling prose.

In his *History of the Dividing Line* he describes the North Carolinians with a contemptuousness that helps explain the animosity these people would hold toward Virginia for generations to come. He wrote of his neighboring state as one where "every one does what seems best in his own eyes. There were some good women that brought their children to be baptized. . . . It was strange that none came to be married in such a multitude. . . . Yet so it was, that though our chaplain christened above an hundred, he did not marry so much as one couple during the whole expedition."

Byrd's descriptions are vivid: "The heavens lowered a little upon us in the Morning, but, like a Damsel ruffled by too bold an Address, soon clear'd." He commented on the innate hospitality of one Virginia district by pointing out that its residents built a church for $50 and a tavern for $500. During a struggle for power with the royal governor, Alexander Spotswood, Byrd wrote that "a man must be either the governor's dog or his ass; neither of which stations suit in the least with my constitution."

Frequently, a single entry in his Diaries will suggest the varied facets of Byrd's life: his reading, his regular exercises (the "dance" to which he refers daily), his frequent marital storms, plantation matters, an extensive social life and personal religious concerns. Thus, the entry for September 1, 1710, reads: "I rose at 5 o'clock and read a chapter in Hebrew and some Greek in Lucian. I said my prayers and ate boiled milk for breakfast. I danced my dance. My wife and I had a quarrel because she neglected to give the child the bitter drink. I settled some accounts. About 11 o'clock Captain Burbydge came and he and I played at billiards. . . . I ate roast pigeon for dinner. . . . Colonel Randolph and Captain Bolling were chosen burgesses for the upper county. My wife and I took a long walk about the plantation. In the evening I read a sermon of Dr. Sacheverell, and had good health, good thoughts, and good humor."

Sut Lovingood, the fictional character through whom east Tennessean George W. Harris related his lusty stories, had almost nothing in common with William Byrd—except an uncommon relish for the pageantry of life. Sut's friends and acquaintances were not the people of the settled and stratified Tidewater; they were the hunters, farmers, fiddlers, sheriffs, lawyers, politicians, preachers and "willin' widders" of the fluid, rowdy frontier. And for his own part, Sut described himself as a "Nat'ral Born Durn'd Fool."

Yet Sut belonged to a tradition, too. From the time of the pioneers' earliest thrust into a harsh, rough wilderness, where simple survival was a triumph and human companionship a luxury, the people of the "western waters" had spun tall tales. At first the stories remained purely verbal, shared at whittling sessions around the crossroads store, on 'coon and 'possum and bear hunts, at camp meetings and militia drills, during house-raisings and cornhuskings and quilting bees, and on court day. Later, some of the yarns were printed, and the popularity of Davy Crockett biographies and "autobiographies" catapulted the extravagant humor of the back country into national prominence. The legend of Crockett the bear hunter, who could "whip his weight in wildcats, grin the bark off an oak-knot—swim further, dive deeper, and come out drier, than any other man in the Western Deestrict," almost obscured the reality of Crockett the Tennessee politician who served in Congress and died at the Alamo.

Sut—whose adventures were published in the years just prior to the Civil War—was not part of the first wilderness. He was part of the transition from rough-hewn countryside to rude village and town, a time when the traits necessary in that earlier period were modified into practical jokes, terrifying tricks and bawdy yarns. Above all, Harris and his fellow humorists are significant because they were some of the earliest realists in American writing. Their characters were the common men and women of Jacksonian democracy. These writers had the qualities of the great truth-stretchers and scamps, of Baron Munchausen and Till Eulenspiegel, yet they did not look back to the Old World but found their characters and situations on native grounds and presented them in native terms. Their influence touched some of our greatest writers, most notably Mark Twain and, more recently, William Faulkner.

Certainly, there are overtones of Huck and Tom and Sid in the opening paragraph of Sut's "Old Skissim's Middle Boy": "When I war a littil over half-grown, hed sprouted my tail feathers, an' wer beginnin tu crow, thar wer a livin in the neighborhood a dredful fat, mean, lazy boy, 'bout my age. He wer the middil son ove a ole lark, name Skissim. He tinkered ontu ole clocks, an' spinin wheels, et lye hominy, an' exhortid at meetin fur a livin, while this middil boy ove hisen did the sleepin fur the hole famurly."

No voice could be more different from this one than that of a near-contemporary of Harris, Edgar Allan Poe. The greatest of all Southern writers and perhaps the most original and tragic talent in American letters, Poe was an isolated literary phenomenon, hungering for a home and yet homeless, wishing to put down roots even as he dreamed of worlds beyond the ken of man.

Born in Boston in 1809, Poe was orphaned at the age of two and unofficially adopted by the John Allan family of Richmond, Virginia. Most of his formative years were spent there and at the University of Virginia at Charlottesville, where his taste for novel reading, poetry writing, gambling and drinking made him the quintessence of the Virginia gentleman. In 1830 Poe's foster father helped him to obtain an appointment to West Point, but he spent more of his time there studying Byron and Coleridge than Caesar and Napoleon. He was dismissed in less than nine months.

Burdened by a succession of lost loves and short-lived editorial positions, ill with drink and drugs, Poe drifted from South to North and back to Baltimore. There he was found dying in the gutter at the age of 40. As his legacy, he left poems like none America had heard before—obscure, ethereal, haunting lyrics that inspired such French poets as Charles Baudelaire and Stéphane Mallarmé. Among them were *tours de force* of versification—such as "The Bells" and "The Raven"—and small classics—"To Helen" and "Annabel Lee."

As a writer of fiction, Poe was probably best known to his contemporaries for his tales of horror—stories like "The Fall of the House of Usher" and "Ligeia," which are aptly described by the title of the collection in which they appeared, *Tales of the Grotesque and Arabesque.* But he also introduced a new form of prose writing, the detective story, exemplified by such classic accounts of detection as "The Purloined Letter" and "The Murders in the Rue Morgue." Poe's was a divided mind, complex and elusive, yet coldly logical and precise. He influenced writers as diverse as Arthur Conan Doyle and Jules Verne, Joseph Conrad and Robert Louis Stevenson.

In both his works and his life, Poe sought a true expression of the Virginia that had adopted him. At a time when American literature was dominated by New England writers in Boston and Concord like Longfellow, Emerson and Thoreau, Poe spoke contemptuously of the "odious old woods of Concord" and the "Frogpondium" of Boston. "I am a Virginian," he said, and he proclaimed that Virginia society was as "absolutely aristocratical as any in Europe." Though he himself neither inherited nor won a place in that society, it remained his image of the good life, and the modern critic Willard Thorp has pointed out that "the traits of the Southern gentleman were exaggerated in Poe almost to the point of burlesque."

It is significant that Poe's strongest influence was felt not in France or in the American North, but in the Border States and the Old South. The Gothic school of Southern writers, including such figures as Carson McCullers and Truman Capote, was born in Poe's "ghoul-haunted woodland of Weir," and Poe's tortured inner vision sank deep

Uniformed Negro students are "at attention" in a class at Virginia's Hampton Institute around the turn of the century. Founded in 1868 by a white man, Samuel Chapman Armstrong, the institute was intended "to train selected Negro youth who should go out and teach and lead their people." From its beginnings in an abandoned Army barracks, Hampton Institute quickly grew into a sizable academy, with a curriculum, often taught by white instructors, that ranged from literature and mathematics to bricklaying and other building trades. Many of the early graduates did become teachers; one of them, Booker T. Washington, went on to found a Negro college, Tuskegee Institute.

into the spirit of the American South as a whole.

To some extent, Poe's mixture of fantasy and horror probably strengthened his influence, for the colonial urbanity of a William Byrd and the antebellum realism of a George Harris found scant echo in the post-Civil War South. In the wake of an actuality that had included death and defeat on hundreds of scarred battlefields within its boundaries, the South retreated to the memory of a time that never was in a never-never-land. The South lost the war but won the national audience, and two of the most popular voices appealing to that audience were from the Border States. Once again they represented the pull between lowland and upland, between an "aristocrat's" and a "commoner's" society. But the disparity between Virginia's Thomas Nelson Page and Tennessee's Mary N. Murfree (better known by her pen name "Charles Egbert Craddock") was not so wide as it might have been, for both were romanticists.

Page, who lived from 1853 to 1922, saw the South turning from its semilegendary image of itself to the crass materialism of its neighbors, and he sought to slow that change by reviving the legend. His most famous story, "Marse Chan," enshrined him in the hearts of all the keepers of the flame for the Lost Cause. In this and his other

tales, Page depicted an idyllic land of columned "Big Houses" and merry slave quarters where faithful retainers refused to desert the old plantation just because of a war and emancipation.

To Page, the life of the antebellum South was the "purest, sweetest life ever lived," and through the faithful ex-slave Sam, he voiced his nostalgia for that life: "Marse Chan . . . sut'n'y wuz good to me. Nothin' nuver made no diffunce 'bout dat. He nuver hit me a lick in his life—an' nuver let nobody else do it, nurr."

Another ex-slave, "Uncle Gabe," expresses his sentiments in verse:

"Fine ole place?" Yes, suh, 't is so;
An' mighty fine people my white folks war—
But you ought ter 'a' seen it years ago,
When de Marster an' de Mistis lived up dyah;
When de niggers 'd stan' all round' de do',
Like grains o' corn on the cornhouse flo'.

This was not only what Southerners wanted to hear but, apparently, what Northerners wanted as well. Having abandoned, to all practical intents and purposes, their avowed crusade for the Negro's liberation, they seemed eager to accept an idealized version of the Old South. The region became the most popular setting in American fiction, and an editor of *Scribner's Monthly* said the South was "in the literary saddle." Page himself told a friend that Boston bought more of his books than did all the state of Virginia.

Nevertheless, Thomas Nelson Page influenced Virginia literature more than anyone of his generation. "His books," says historian Marshall W. Fishwick, "are Virginian to the core," and Fishwick suggests that "anyone who wants to understand the working of the Virginia mind, and the persistence of certain attitudes into the twentieth century," should read the collection of stories *In Ole Virginia*. As recently as 1960, the North Carolina historian and biographer Gerald W. Johnson asserted that Thomas Nelson Page and composer Stephen Foster had proved to be greater enemies of the South than Generals Grant or Sherman, for they "propagated a titanic lie."

At the opposite end of the "local color" spectrum, in her characters if not in her personal background, was Mary N. Murfree. As Charles Egbert Craddock, she gained wide national popularity. (The editor of *The Atlantic Monthly,* Thomas Bailey Aldrich, published her work for years before he discovered that this "man" was really the fragile daughter of a central Tennessee plantation family.) During summer visits to the Cumberland Mountains, Mary Murfree became familiar with the mountain people, who have been, according to the literary historian Jay B. Hubbell, "more misrepresented in American fiction than the people of any other Southern region—and that is saying a good deal."

Miss Murfree did not altogether correct the misrepresentations, but in her widely read novels —notably *The Prophet of the Great Smoky Mountains* and *In the "Stranger People's" Country*—she lifted mountain people from caricatures to characters. In the words of one critic, she "revealed . . . the pathos of the lonely, frustrated lives of the mountaineers and the solemn poetic beauty of their surroundings." And the dialect of her characters is "faithfully reproduced, with its dry caustic wit and drawling intonations."

By 1900 Mary Murfree's early and enormous success was fading. New voices were rising in the Border States—writers skeptical or contemptuous of the myths of the past, and free of the old allegiances to the Tidewater or the back country. The first of them was the novelist Ellen Glasgow. No one could have suspected that the significant break with Victorian sentimentality and local color in Southern literature would come through the

work of an aristocratic, privately educated, formally presented young lady. Yet when her earliest works appeared, according to one observer, "realism crossed the Potomac, . . . going North!"

After the publication in 1897 of her first novel, *The Descendant,* Ellen Glasgow said, "I had made my break for good and all; I was free." So was the literature of the Border States and the South in a way that it had not been for a long time. Her central character was a poor white, and illegitimate. Miss Glasgow disregarded her relatives' pleas, "If you must write, do write of Southern ladies and gentlemen," and felt that she was "beginning a solitary revolt against the formal, the false, the affected, the sentimental, and the pretentious in Southern writing." She reflected a new critical attitude toward life in the Border States when she said that "the Southerner learned to read, to write and to preach before he learned to think—there was, indeed, no need for thinking when everybody thought alike, or, rather, when to think differently meant to be ostracized."

"What the South needs is blood and irony," said Ellen Glasgow, and she provided healthy transfusions of both. Her characters—neither idealized aristocrats nor depraved primitives— were generally middle class or poor white, and defied stereotyped categories. Her novels penetrated much of the sham and hypocrisy of Virginia society to portray the tension between accumulated tradition and pressing change. In *Virginia* she described her genteel heroine as one whose "education was founded upon the simple theory that the less a girl knew about life, the better prepared she would be to contend with it." In a later novel, *One Man in His Time,* she wrote of a character named Stephen Culpeper: "Democracy, relentless, disorderly, and strewn with the wreckage of finer things, had overwhelmed the world of established customs in which he lived."

In her best-known book, *Barren Ground,* Miss Glasgow created one of the distinctive characters of Border States—and American—fiction. The heroine, Dorinda Oakley, fulfills the author's intention to "portray not Southern 'types' alone, but whole human beings," as she learns to "live gallantly, without delight." The setting for Dorinda's fortitude vividly captures one of the region's characteristic scenes, with "the houses, the roads, the woods, the endless fields of broomsedge and scrub pine, the low, immeasurable horizon," which Miss Glasgow had known since childhood. "And while the wind bewitched the solitude, a vague restless-

The divided crusaders

RUPERT B. VANCE

W. J. CASH

HOWARD W. ODUM

In the 1920s and early 1930s, the Border States produced two opposing schools of writers and thinkers, the "agrarians" and the "regionalists." The agrarians advocated the decentralization of government and a return to an agricultural society. Their leaders, shown at right in a 1956 reunion, first assembled at Vanderbilt University in Nashville Tennessee. There they briefly published *The Fugitive*, a notable literary magazine.

The champions of regionalism *(left)*, centered at the University of North Carolina, countered with calls for what spokesman Howard W. Odum described as "an effective balance between uncontrolled individualism among the states and complete centralization . . . at Washington."

Both groups eventually disintegrated as the passage of time rendered their arguments little more than academic.

ness would stir in the hearts of living things on the farms, of men, women and animals. 'Broomsage ain't jest wild stuff. It's a kind of fate,' old Matthew Fairlamb used to say."

In many of her 23 published books she paid tribute to the region's "vein of iron"—the "Scottish strain of fortitude that has come down from the earliest pioneers in the [Shenandoah] Valley." The violence and gentleness that have co-existed in the Border States were understood and beautifully set forth in her creation of General David Archbald in *The Sheltered Life*. At one point in the story, General Archbald meditates on his grandfather's love of the hunt: "For nothing escaped his knife or his gun, not the mole in the earth, not the lark in the air. He could no more look at a wild creature without lusting to kill than he could look at a pretty girl without lusting to kiss." To the shame of his family, General Archbald himself, as a boy, did not want to be a hunter, but a poet. At 83, "the poet in him . . . lost," he reviews his life as a military man, prosperous attorney and member of the Episcopal Church. Reflecting upon values he had lived by, he concludes that he "had had a fair life. Nothing that he wanted, but everything that was good for him."

Values—abiding and decaying, in disarray and

transition—were also the major concern of a group of literary figures who gathered in the 1920s at Vanderbilt University in Nashville, Tennessee. Eventually called "the Fugitives," after the magazine that they initiated in April 1922, the group occupied a middle ground between "a sentimentalized South and a commercialized South." Their mentor was the poet and critic John Crowe Ransom, then of the university's English department; other members of the original group included Allen Tate, Donald Davidson, Merrill Moore and Robert Penn Warren.

The Fugitives rejected both the memory of legendary magnolias and the modern faith in science. Allen Tate summed up the nature of their vision: "With the war of 1914-1918, the South reentered the world—but gave a backward glance as it stepped over the border: that backward glance gave us the Southern renascence, a literature conscious of the past in the present." They themselves helped to nurture that renascence in *The Fugitive* magazine. "Had any little literary magazine before or since," asks literary critic Louis D. Rubin Jr., "contained so much talent on its editorial board? Had the pages of any other little magazine contained as many poems still read and admired decades afterward?"

ALLEN TATE   MERRILL MOORE   ROBERT PENN WARREN   JOHN CROWE RANSOM   DONALD DAVIDSON

But the young Fugitives soon concluded that their chief antagonist was the future—that "up-to-date" world of undirected change. Their magazine disappeared in 1925 and they eventually dissolved into another group, one that had a stronger voice —a voice that played a part in a major confrontation in the intellectual life of the Border States.

In 1930 there appeared a book which marked the rise of two contrasting and controversial philosophies. These philosophies, agrarianism and regionalism, had their deepest roots and fullest development in the Border States. Agrarianism, which enlisted the services of many of the old Fugitive group, was centered around Vanderbilt University in Nashville; regionalism, which called for social and economic progress under the aegis of large-scale planning, flourished at the University of North Carolina at Chapel Hill. These two views of past and present, with their conflicting guidelines for future directions, once again revealed the divided mind of the Border States. The debate between agrarianism and regionalism was in large measure a debate that concerned all the states, for it posed questions pertinent to the whole nation's future.

The book constituting the agrarian manifesto was *I'll Take My Stand; The South and the Agrar-ian Tradition,* a symposium in which twelve writers rejected certain aspects of American progress and reaffirmed certain spiritual needs. Their ideal was the small, independent farmer, proud and self-sufficient, who was to be developed as an individual rather than used as a robot. This vision ran head-on into the region's ambition to secure bigger and better industries as one means of pulling out of a grinding poverty.

The agrarians who took their stand included four of the original Fugitives—Ransom, Tate, Davidson and Warren—and four other literary figures: Andrew Nelson Lytle, Stark Young, John Gould Fletcher and John Donald Wade. The views of this group—which also included a political scientist, a journalist and a psychologist—were greeted as audacious—or outrageous. They were denounced as "young Confederates," and North Carolina-born Gerald W. Johnson asked, "Have they never been in the modern south . . . ? Are they unaware of pellagra and hookworm, two flowers of Southern agrarianism?" It was this gap between the vision and the reality that made the agrarians often seem to be "the champions of a second Lost Cause."

No one could discount the talent in their ranks, however. Through them the Border States found especially important voices, particularly in the poetry of Kentucky-born Allen Tate and Tennessean John Crowe Ransom. And after he left their fold, Robert Penn Warren went on to become the most wide-ranging and significant artist of the lot. In poetry, criticism and fiction he examined ancient dilemmas and current crises. His long poem, *The Ballad of Billie Potts,* captured the zest and adventure and "gore-blood" mystery that haunted much of the Border States' voice. *Night Rider,* his first novel, dramatized the Black Patch tobacco wars of his native Kentucky, using the interplay of past and present to enrich character and situation. In his best-known novel, *All The King's Men,* based on the story of the demagogue Huey Long, Warren was "concerned with the human position, which is to say, with the plight of men caught in the dilemma between absolute moral ideals and the demands of the immediate, 'real' world." Warren had the ability to focus that dilemma in sharp conflicts and reconciliations.

In condemning Northeastern financial domination, outsiders' misconceptions and sociological oversimplifications, the agrarian who persisted longest was poet and polemicist Donald Davidson. He denounced those who thought the Southern farmer "gullied and exhausted his lands" because "he was a limb of Satan" rather than because he was in thrall to Northern imperialists. Discussing sociology, Davidson sharpened his finest sarcasm and revealed a deeply racist aspect of his position. "For better or worse," he wrote, "the sociologist has become the chief expert consultant on the Negro problem, at least to that part of the American public which believes that the problem can be solved by legislative means. The reasoning of this public can be briefly stated as follows: The cause of the problem is race prejudice, which is a kind of social disease afflicting white folks, especially in the South; the sociologist is a kind of doctor, who isolates and describes the disease, and then designates remedy and treatment; apply remedy and treatment through Federal legislation, and you have the cure." The tenacity of his views is illustrated by the title of his book, *Still Rebels, Still Yankees,* published as late as 1957.

Davidson stood opposed to the regionalists, the other major group voicing a philosophy for the Border States during this period. As an agrarian, he rejected "education to cure 'ignorance' and 'prejudice'; factories to cure poverty; and more and bigger laws, bureaus, and governments to do away with social 'injustice.'" The regionalists, on the other hand, were characterized precisely by their belief in education, factories, social legislation and many other institutions of improvement.

Howard W. Odum, the central figure of the Chapel Hill group, said that the region should be studied by social scientists who were thoroughly objective yet touched by the compassion of poetry. He assembled a dynamic and able group of young researchers and writers to help create a regionalism that "would promote integration of the region into the nation, permitting diversity, but only in a larger framework of the national welfare." Their studies of racial, economic and social needs and solutions produced a rich and unique body of documentary literature. Among the earliest of these books were Rupert B. Vance's *Human Factors in Cotton Culture* and *Human Geography of the South,* which combined the cold statistics of an economy with the warm flesh of its society.

The book which became the Bible of the regionalists was Odum's *Southern Regions of the United States.* It was an exhaustive compendium of facts, figures and charts, combined with a detailed statement of the region's problems and potentials. The planning it tentatively suggested and defined never materialized, but its impact was a major one; in the words of historian George B. Tindall, "Odum's chief contribution was that he, like the Agrarians, provided the impetus of an idea." Tindall also sums up each of these two influential and contrasting movements which came out of the Border States: "Agrarianism quickened a generation of writers with its vision of Southern tradition beset by change. Regionalism quickened a generation of social scientists with its vision of the 'problem South,' a region with obvious deficiencies but with potentialities that demanded constructive study and planning."

Tradition and change: the voices of the Border States expressed the whole spectrum. One regional classic probed for an understanding of the dichotomy. It was *The Mind of the South,* by a newspaperman from Charlotte, North Carolina, W. J. Cash. When the book appeared in 1941 *The Atlantic Monthly* hailed it as a "literary and moral miracle." George Tindall has called it "the product of exhaustive reading, perceptive observation, and a creative insight that transcended the limitations of his own and the historian's professions."

Cash's combination of eloquence and simplicity, sympathy and anger, the historical and the personal, illuminated many areas of Southern thought and action. His own experience of the

South was gained in the Border States, and he drew deeply upon that experience to convey the intangible influences shaping the Southern mind. In a single sentence he was able to evoke place and mood: "There are days when the booming of the wind in the pines is like the audible rushing of time—when the sad knowledge of the grave stirs in the subconsciousness and bends the spirit to melancholy, days when the questions that have no answers must insinuate themselves into the minds of the least analytical of men." But he also displayed the wry iconoclasm characteristic of so many Border States' voices: "If one is to maintain that the ruling class of the great South was really an aristocracy, one must suppose that it somehow rose up from the frontier and got to be such in forty or fifty years at best."

They were non-fiction interpretations, those regional studies. But a powerful achievement in fiction also came forth from North Carolina during these years, to give natives and strangers alike a new awareness of the region and of themselves. One critic called Thomas Wolfe's *Look Homeward, Angel* "the nearest thing to a literary thunderbolt in the 20th Century."

Appropriately, the thunderbolt came from the mountains. Wolfe was born and reared in Asheville, North Carolina. His father was a native of Pennsylvania; his mother's ancestry was deeply rooted in the Appalachians. Like so many Border States figures, he was a man of contradictions. His literary romanticism (which has been thoroughly deplored) contrasted with his satiric realism (which has been infrequently recognized); and one of the persistent tensions in his personal life was between the petty, restricted, suffocating life of a mountain town and the dark, impersonal fury of the metropolis. But he told Maxwell Perkins, his editor, "The people of North Carolina are like that wonderful earth. . . . I am going to *tell the truth* about these people and, by God, it is the truth about America."

From the moment of publication of *Look Homeward, Angel* in 1929, when Wolfe was 29 years old, his work aroused storms of argument. To some critics and readers his outpouring of words, his adolescent anguish and the paradoxes of his character were insufferable. To others, his rhapsodic hymns to seasons and trains and man's everlasting loneliness were unforgettable. Wolfe was called a "young Werther," after Goethe's self-pitying, long-suffering hero, and he was also compared to Homer; he was dismissed as an undisci-

Novelist Thomas Wolfe sits with his mother on the porch of the boardinghouse in Asheville, North Carolina, where he lived as a child. In his brief career—he died in 1938, at the age of 38—Wolfe produced a body of work, largely about his native town, that won the praise of such literary figures as William Faulkner —who ranked him first among modern American writers.

plined rustic and celebrated as a prophetic poet.

Despite the critical dispute over his genius or lack of it, Wolfe's work found readers. None of his novels has ever gone out of print, neither the two published before his death in 1938, *Look Homeward, Angel* and *Of Time and the River,* nor the two pieced together by an editor after his death, *The Web and the Rock* and *You Can't Go Home Again.* In 1967 *Look Homeward, Angel* alone sold 55,000 copies. And William Faulkner, perhaps the greatest of his contemporaries, put Wolfe at the head of the list of modern American novelists (in the place just ahead of himself) because Wolfe "made the best failure," and "tried his best to get it all said."

If Wolfe did not say it all, he said a great deal, and he captured as did no one else the essence of his region's countryside and town, mountaineers and middle class, terror and tomfoolery. Here, for example, is his celebration of autumn: "Now October has come again which in our land is different from October in the other lands. The ripe, the golden month has come again, and in Virginia the chinkapins are falling. Frost sharps the middle music of the seasons, and all things living on the earth turn home again. . . .

"October is the richest of the seasons: the fields

are cut, the granaries are full, the bins are loaded to the brim with fatness, and from the cider-press the rich brown oozings of the York Imperials run. The bee bores to the belly of the yellowed grape, the fly gets old and fat and blue, he buzzes loud, crawls slow, creeps heavily to death on sill and ceiling, the sun goes down in blood and pollen across the bronzed and mown fields."

He could draw on buried folk memory and factual history to conjure up the past in a single vivid sentence: "In red-oak thickets, at the break of day, long hunters lay for bear." In the short story "Chickamauga," an old man relives a day in a cedar grove when he met the reality of war and the strangeness of death and survival. Wolfe's awareness of the presence of the past in the Border States is expressed in an account of a group of friends from a university in the North Carolina Piedmont who travel to Richmond for a football game: "They felt in touch with wonder and with life, they felt in touch with magic and with history. They saw the state house and they heard the guns. They knew that Grant was pounding at the gates of Richmond. They knew that Lee was digging in some twenty miles away at Petersburg. . . . They knew that Jubal Early was swinging in his saddle at the suburbs of Washington. They felt, they knew, they had their living hands and hearts upon the living presence of these things, and upon a thousand other things as well."

According to critic Maxwell Geismar, the hill people portrayed by Wolfe had a mixture "not so noticeable in the Mississippi deltas or in the Georgia pinelands—of primitive myth *and* equalitarian enlightenment; of voodoo *and* the bill of rights." Perhaps it was the mixture of these qualities in his own personality that kept Wolfe independent of both the cynics and the expatriates of his times. But this did not mean that Wolfe was blind to the world around him. His fiction is filled with scenes and conversations of such authenticity that only an artist with the keenest eye and ear and total powers of concentration and memory could absorb them and then render them into literature. In his autobiographical fiction, he often made himself seem larger than life, but he also made the life of the Border States—and of New York, or Europe, or wherever he lived and traveled—carry meaning beyond any provincial limitations.

In *You Can't Go Home Again,* for example, Wolfe ranged with stunning accuracy and anger from portraying a Southern judge who built a fortune on the sweat-stained dollars and ignorant fears of Negroes in his debt, to showing the total obscenity of a Nazi bully holding a nameless, terrified Jewish man in his power. Wolfe had met the Jewish victim as a fellow passenger on a train, and his account of this revelation of the sinister savagery of the rising Nazis was published in *The New Republic* in 1936, and later in his final novel. Each betrayal of justice, in the Border States or in Germany, mocked the credo Wolfe had written for the protean country he strove to encompass and interpret: "So, then, to every man his chance—to every man, regardless of his birth, his shining, golden opportunity—to every man the right to live, to work, to be himself, and to become whatever thing his manhood and his vision can combine to make him—this, seeker, is the promise of America."

This was the old spoken magic of the Border States, rising from the mountains of Wolfe's Asheville to embody all men's hope.

It is little wonder that Wolfe's prose frequently had a bardic quality. He was born of a people who had been telling their chronicles, singing their history, for generations. And during the years when Wolfe's novels were appearing, one of the Border States' unique contributions to American culture was emerging into the national consciousness: folk music.

While literary romanticists and realists were presenting alternate views of the Border States' unreconstructed gentility and rampant squalor, two of the submerged groups in the region went ahead singing in their own indigenous voices. Through long ancestries, among isolated mountaineers and among subject Negroes, there had grown a strong simple music, its roots deep in the past, its appeal universal.

In 1917 the English folk-song collector, Cecil Sharp, said after a visit to the Appalachian Mountains of the Border States: "I found myself for the first time in my life in a community in which singing was as common and almost as universal a practice as speaking"—and the singing had preserved intact many of the old songs of his native land. Sharp had been attracted to the Southern hills by Olive Dame Campbell, a New England schoolteacher whose work with her husband, John C. Campbell, led to an important study, *The Southern Highlander and His Homeland,* and to the establishment of the John C. Campbell Folk School at Brasstown, North Carolina. Mrs. Campbell journeyed from North Carolina to Massachusetts to talk with Sharp, carrying the notebook in which she had recorded a haunting version of that best known of all ballads, "Barbara Allen," sung by a pupil at the Hindman Settlement School in Kentucky.

Other teachers and collectors who came to explore and preserve the music of the mountains were often struck by the attitude of the music-makers. Thus, B. A. Botkin was told by one man: "I'm a fiddler, you know, not a violinist. What I play is old-time stuff. I don't know a thing about music." The point was that his music was not a separate part of the mountain man's life; it was as nourishing and necessary as daily bread. But it was also the vehicle of a strong and enduring tradition. A North Carolina folklorist, Richard Chase, summarized the meaning and method of this folklore when he stated, "It is only when our old songs and old tales are passing from one human being to another, by word-of-mouth, that they can attain their full fascination. No printed page can create this spell. It is the living word—the sung ballad and the told tale—that holds our attention and reaches our hearts."

In their ballads, the mountain people preserved memories of comely lords and ladies ("Lord Lovel," "Fair Margaret and Sweet William," "Lord Thomas and Fair Ellen"), recounted tragedies and disasters ("The Doom of Floyd Collins"), celebrated Christmas and their religious hungers ("I Wonder As I Wander"), and recorded the bittersweet anguish of lost or unrequited love. Some of their songs carried on the age-old tradition of Scottish balladry:

> *Where have you been all this day,*
> *Randal, oh, my son?*
> *Where have you been all this day,*
> *My sweet and pretty one?*
> *…Mother, make my bed soon,*
> *I'm sick to the heart,*
> *And fain would lie down.*

But not all of the songs were of long-past events or distant places. "If I Had A Ribbon-Bow" voiced a very modern longing:

> *And when he goes to Frankfort,*
> *a-loggin' on the rise,*
> *He'll bring me back with his own hands,*
> *a very pretty prize. . . .*
> *Then I'd live in Frankfort,*
> *where all the lawin' goes,*
> *I'd lark about them settlements,*
> *and wear them furrin clothes.*

Those who searched out these ballads often came in contact with the atmosphere and surroundings from which the ballads had grown. One young collector described such experiences: "I remember young Jeff Breeden calling out the figures for the dance in his father's cabin, where the stove had been taken down to make room for the dancers who had traveled 'clean across the mountain for the gatherin'. I can see old Scritch Breeden, his chair tipped against the wall, fiddling 'Locks and Bolts Can't Keep Love Out.' I remember Hastings Taylor singing, 'Don't Never Let Your Woman Have Her Way,' as he let the Mission Lady and me trail along after him on a Possum Hunt and pick ourselves up when we came a-cropper trying to cross a stream by the means of taking a flying leap on a wild grape vine. I remember pretty Missy Breeden singing, 'The Light-haired Lover' as we strung peppers and shelled walnuts by her mother's hearth. I can still smell the wood smoke and see the shadowy figures moving about the fire in Old Man Oby's yard on an autumn evening."

The ballads have journeyed out of the lonely little coves and rocky creek-bottoms to capture the rest of the country with their sincerity and freshness. Thin and high as wind in the reeds, rich and full as corn-shocked fields in autumn, the voices have emerged: "Doc" Watson from Deep Gap, where the mountains of Virginia, Tennessee and North Carolina meet—blind, yet seeing to the heart of a song with guitar or banjo or his deep voice; sweet-toned Jean Ritchie, who brought the music of her childhood home in Viper, Kentucky, and her family of 13 brothers and sisters to a larger world; Pleaz Mobley and Virgil Sturgill and Billy Edd Wheeler, whose talents have recorded old and new songs from their knowledge of Kentucky and North Carolina and West Virginia; rugged Frank Proffitt, who sang a song called "Tom Dula" which became the Kingston Trio's "Tom Dooley," who once described himself as "to some extent flesh and much bone," and who summarized in a letter to a recording company the spirit of the best of the ballad singers: "While I know I am not much, musically speaking, I do what I am able, trying to keep to the original as handed to me from other days. I know I am not being paid for musical talent or for things I have done, but only for what was 'give' to me. I think of my father who sang and told me of the old days as he heard it. He lived and died perhaps never having $250 at one time in his whole life. When you realize how undeserving

I know I am of the many recognitions now coming my way, you then can imagine how my gratefulness is a thing that goes very deep."

In 1943 the collector and singer John Jacob Niles prophesied of the mountain ballads: "Hundreds of years from now, these mountains will still stand, silent brooding masses. The slag-piles will be overgrown, the boom-towns forgotten, the coal-tipples tumbled into dust, and the family wars fought out and forgotten—but, if the present trend prevails, the folk music of today, much of which is now four centuries old, will prevail then and will be as precious to the masses in that far future time as it is to a relatively few students and enthusiasts today." It is already clear that Niles may have been a better prophet than he realized. Today, only a single generation since he made his statement, masses of people in the United States can attest to the truth of his vision.

Somewhere between the mountaineers' ballads and the folk songs of the Negroes is "Casey Jones," handed down from the great days of railroading. The black-haired, daring six-foot-four-inch engineer who lived in Jackson, Tennessee, midway between the mountains and the Mississippi, saved the life of his fireman at the loss of his own on April 29, 1906, when he called out, "Boy, you better jump, 'Cause there's two locomotives that's a-goin' to bump." Casey Jones's song was first "made up" by a Negro engine wiper, Wallace Saunders, and it has been sung during the decades since in numerous versions.

True Negro folk songs, such as "John Henry," deal more directly with the submerged life of the Negro people. The saga of this "steel-drivin' man," who helped build the Big Bend Tunnel on the Chesapeake and Ohio Railroad line, has everything: the harsh labor of opening up the Border States, the competition between man and the machine, the triumph of spirit over physical death.

> *John Henry told his captain*
> *A man ain't nothin' but a man;*
> *Before I let that steam drill beat me down,*
> *I'll die with my hammer in my hand.*

In the judgment of many, no native ballad is more memorable.

And there are still other forms of Negro folk music. The spirituals, giving voice to the abject misery and triumphant hope of an indestructible people, come mainly from the lowland reaches of the Border States. But a special musical contribution of the river deltas and fertile flatlands origi-

nated in a single city, Memphis. The city on the bluff above the Mississippi was the center of a plantation area; in addition, it always had a large Negro population. From the "work songs" of the field hands and the "lonesome songs" of the townspeople, came a music called "the blues," first written down and published by a man named W. C. Handy. His earliest success, "The Memphis Blues," was written in 1909 and published three years later. Later Handy songs included the "Beale Street Blues" and the biggest of all his hits, the classic "St. Louis Blues."

A student of the blues, John F. Szwed, has described the highly personal quality of this music as it developed through the years: "Emotionally charged, deeply personalized, the blues were in part a problem-solving technique, closer to the confessional than to the stage. The blues audience responded to the common plights presented to them by the singer as personal experience. As the singer overcame his problems, or was overcome by them, so the listeners shared in the catharsis." In the years after World War II, it "was Memphis, Tennessee, that seemed to be the new center of blues . . . . Singers such as Gatemouth Moore and Johnny Ace, and later, Bobby Bland and B. B. King set the style of blues that remains most popular with younger Negroes today." And Szwed points out that the phenomenally successful rock 'n' roll of Elvis Presley, whose home is in Memphis, emulates "the spirit (and sometimes even the letter) of urban blues."

W. C. Handy once said, "Southern Negroes sang about everything. Trains, steamboats, steam whistles, sledge hammers, fast women, mean bosses, stubborn mules—all became subjects for their songs. They accompany themselves on anything from which they can extract a musical sound or rhythmical effect, anything from a harmonica to a washboard. In this way, and from these materials, they set the mood for what we now call blues."

In a way, Handy's description applies to all the music and literature of the Border States. Renowned or anonymous, the creative artists who wrote the books and composed the songs of the region seized upon an enormous range of subject matter. Through art, and with these materials, they set a mood and created both an outer and an inner landscape that fully expressed the life of their place and time. And their work has traveled far beyond the place of its making, to enlighten and entertain the people of their nation and the world.

Performers gather before Nashville's Country Music Hall of Fame, built in 1966.

The mighty "Nashville Sound"

Almost 1,000 miles from Broadway, more than 2,000 miles from Hollywood, central Tennessee seems remote from the world of show business. But that is where Nashville is, and Nashville is where the action is in popular music. The center of a $100 million music industry, it produces nearly half of America's popular records, mainly in a complex style called the "Nashville Sound." The source and main ingredient of the "Sound" is country music— an informal, sometimes comic, style brought to the city in the mid-1920s. Today, music is produced in Nashville by a host of musicians, song writers, record companies and music publishers, and it has rewarded many of them lavishly. Almost every day a star like Perry Como or Connie Francis joins local musicians in a Nashville studio. In a short time a record is made and, through the alchemy of the Nashville Sound, the strum of guitars and twang of banjos is transmuted into the rustle of dollar bills

Photographs by Jerry Cooke

Country-music performers chat and walk about the stage during the weekly broadcast of *Grand Ole Opry (left)*. Keeping track of all the confused goings-on is the job of coordinators like the girl at the desk in the foreground.

Cousin Minnie Pearl *(right)*, an off-stage millionairess, exemplifies the homespun flavor of *Grand Ole Opry* as she barks her famous "How-DEE! I'm just so proud to be here" to her millions of fans throughout the country.

The grand old "Grand Ole Opry"

Every Saturday about noon in Nashville, men, women and children begin to line up for the broadcast of *Grand Ole Opry,* a homespun radio show that has been described as "a mixture of chaos and corn," but has proved astonishingly durable and influential. By show time at 7:30 the assembled fans, who travel an average of 500 miles to watch their favorite *Opry* stars perform, number about 5,000—and some 10 million people are tuned in throughout the United States.

Grand Ole Opry is an informal mixture of music, comedy and free-for-all fun-making; in the course of the broadcast, the performers, their families and their friends mill around the stage, creating a background of utter disorder for the performers at stage center. Yet no radio show has ever had a greater impact upon the city of its birth. The *Opry* is the oldest established radio program in the United States (it first went on the air November 28, 1925), and it has made Nashville the country-music center of the entire nation. What is more important, *Opry* musicians, always in demand as accompanists and composers, have attracted scores of recording companies and music publishers to the city. Over the years, the homespun sound of *Grand Ole Opry* has been a major ingredient of the Nashville Sound.

Backwoods humor is dispensed by James C. Summey, known to country-music fans as "Cousin Jody," who takes his turn at the *Opry* microphone wearing his trademark, a squashed hat, and playing a battered guitar he calls his "biscuit board."

Country-style pickin' and singin'

From its beginnings to the present day, country music has been dominated by the sounds of plucked instruments, particularly the guitar (now often electrically amplified) and the banjo. These instruments provide the background for most of the music performed in Nashville today, but they figure most prominently in older and simpler musical styles. Virtuoso guitar playing is part of the act in the down-home humor of performers like Homer and Jethro *(below)*, and both guitar and banjo form the basis of "Bluegrass," a largely improvised, jazzy style of country music that dates back to 19th Century banjo and fiddle duets. No Bluegrass band has won more popularity among urban and rural audiences than that of Lester Flatt, Earl Scruggs and the Foggy Mountain Boys *(right)*, sparked by the lightning-fast banjo picking of Earl Scruggs, who has been called the "Paganini of the banjo."

Homer *(left)* and Jethro record a parody of a "pop" tune at Nashville's Underwood Auditorium.

Flatt *(left)* and Scruggs are caught by a fish-eye lens at one of Nashville's landmarks—a full-scale replica of the Parthenon.

"Class" guitar with a country flavor

No one has done more to develop the rich complexities of the Nashville Sound out of the simplicities of country music than the recording artist and executive Chet Atkins. Largely through his influence, the old country music, with its narrow appeal to rural audiences, has evolved into a broad-based mixture of styles that is popular both in this country and abroad. As an

Chet Atkins participates in a recording session in Nashville.

observer at Nashville's first Country Music Festival said, "Chet Atkins made country music respectable."

It is significant that, unlike most makers of the Nashville Sound, Atkins is a sophisticated musician. Born in the Clinch Mountains of east Tennessee in 1924, he settled in Nashville in 1950. Since then, he has provided guitar accompaniments for such stars as Elvis Presley, Eddy Arnold and the late Hank Williams, and has recorded a large repertory of music by composers ranging from Bach to the Beatles; he also appears regularly as a guest soloist with symphony orchestras. In 1957 Atkins became head of the Nashville office of RCA Victor, which now records about 45 per cent of the popular music in "Music City."

A multiple exposure catches Atkins with an array of awards for his hit records.

The high lives of the stars

Money, as well as entertainment, has been a major end product of the Nashville Sound; money for song writers, for record companies, for music publishers, and, most of all, for singers and musicians. Many country-music performers have come to Nashville from poverty-stricken backwoods existences and, after the success of a few records, have amassed fortunes that

Webb Pierce stands before his guitar-shaped swimming pool.

support lives of comfort and luxury. Singer Eddy Arnold, the "Tennessee Plowboy" who once serenaded his mule at the end of a day's work in the fields, now wears British tweed jackets and imported Italian shoes, and has vast real-estate holdings. Singer Roger Miller was an elevator operator in Nashville before his overnight success; Webb Pierce (below) was once a Sears Roebuck clerk in Shreveport, Louisiana. Many of these stars have celebrated their successes with zestful extravagance. Wide-brimmed Stetsons, ornate hand-tooled boots and suits studded with rhinestones are common in Nashville, and some country-music stars boast of handmade mother-of-pearl guitars, newly built mansions and enormous "spreads" of blooded cattle.

Pierce's convertible has genuine pistols on dashboard and doors, a bullet-studded steering wheel and leather surfaces set with silver dollars.

8

Patterns of Change

They tell the story in the Border States of an old east Tennessee mountain man whose farm, handed down from great-grandfather and grandfather and father, was bought by the Great Smoky Mountains National Park. "It is progress," he was told. He moved out, bought a little tract of river-bottom land and had settled down again when TVA began construction of a new dam and government agents told him his acres would be covered with water and he would have to move. "It's progress," they explained. He moved again, bought another plot of ground and was just bringing it under cultivation when the engineers for a new interstate highway informed him the road would cut right through the middle of his farm. "It's progress," they said. And the farmer sighed, "Well, I'll sure be glad when this progress is finished. It's damned near ruint me!"

If that farmer ever existed, he knew how "progress" could affect the life and work of one man in the Border States. Other kinds of progress, slower and more subtle in their operation, have affected

farms and farmers throughout the region. Consider, for example, the case of the lowly mule—or, more accurately, the disappearing mule. In the early 1940s there were some 14 million horses and mules in the United States, and the majority of them were in the Border States. More than a quarter of a million mules were on Tennessee farms alone, and Columbia, south of Nashville, was one of the region's largest mule-trading centers.

Mules had been a part of Kentucky life since George Washington encouraged their use by importing jacks from Europe and sending them on a breeding tour of the region. Henry Clay, who also imported European jacks, furthered the mule industry in Kentucky to such an extent that other leading states, especially Tennessee and Missouri, obtained their breeding stock from Kentucky. Before World War II, in Murray, Kentucky, the fourth Monday in March was Mule Trading Day, when buyers and sellers from the surrounding countryside came to dicker or merely to look. Mayfield was an even larger "mule swapping" center. Once a year the street around the Mayfield public square was converted into a "ring" for farmers and mule traders, where speculators compared and bargained and exchanged everything from mules and tall tales to pocketknives and political pre-

Years after strip miners ripped away the ground to get at seams of coal beneath, a once fertile forestland in Kentucky lies eroded and barren. The state now requires miners to post bonds covering the cost of restoring strip-mined land.

155

dictions. A man's success as a farmer, his status as a landowner or renter or sharecropper, was reflected in the quality of his mules. As with so many other resources, the best mules were to be found on large plantations, while the smallest, poorest ones usually belonged to Negro sharecroppers, especially in the Bright Leaf tobacco and the cotton country. To pull an infirm animal through a hard winter, from one harvest to the next planting, was often a major victory, spelling the difference between profit and disaster on the year's crop.

Within two short decades, however, there were few mules left; by the early 1960s most census reports, including the statistical tables of the *World Almanac*, did not even record their number. Horses still flourish, of course, on the Bluegrass farms of Kentucky and Tennessee and in the famous riding and hunt country of North Carolina and Virginia, but the mule—once an everyday necessity, the muscle of the poor man's farm and the rich man's plantation—has become a rarity.

As the mule fades from the Border States, a way of life vanishes too. The machine that does the work of several mules consumes no grass or corn or hay, so the crops on the farms change. Other changes are less obvious. A man operating a machine moves at a different pace, and has a different relationship with the ground, the seasons and the harvests than one who works with a mule. Of all draft animals the mule is reputedly the most cantankerous and individualistic, albeit sturdy and hard-working when it chooses. Working a mule required a special language that made up in vigor what it lacked in nicety. Trading a mule developed a talent for arranging facts that made a successful practitioner the equal of today's United Nations diplomat. Daily dependence on a mule brought realization of the hazards and uncertainties of life and let a man know that he was only one of many creatures necessary to nature's design.

The disappearing mule is taking a number of sights and institutions into oblivion. Gone with the cantankerous animal are the blacksmith shop, the crossroads feed store, the veterinarian's stable and, above all, the annual swapping site—all abandoned or unrecognizably altered, along with the sociability they fostered. Once they were gathering places for long, leisurely talk. The range of conversation in the modern filling station often seems to be encompassed by "Fill her up" and "Where's the green stamps?"

If the shift from mule to machine spanned several decades, other changes in the Border States

have been dramatically swift. Of them all, perhaps none was more significant than that symbolized by the creation, in the war years of 1943 to 1945, of an entire city at the Black Oak Ridge in Tennessee. The very circumstances in which the new city had its beginnings were strangely ominous. There were generals from Washington, scientists with odd difficult names from nations "across the waters," administrators and engineers and personnel men drawn from all parts of the country. High priorities made all necessary materials readily available and buildings sprang up like mushrooms after rain. There were boxlike barracks for construction workers, hastily assembled houses and apartments for professional men, long anonymous laboratories and a great central building encased in black sheet iron. There were miles of forbidding fences, and there was mud when it rained, choking dust when it was dry. Suddenly there was a city. On the Black Oak Ridge, about 18 miles northwest of Knoxville, where there had been only trees and fields and scattered farmhouses a few months before, a secret city—Oak Ridge—had come into existence.

The Border States had experienced the rapid growth of towns before. In West Virginia, for instance, between 1891 and 1900, cornfields gave way

Nestled in the pine-covered hills of eastern Tennessee lies the nation's first uranium purifying plant, the electromagnetic separation division at Oak Ridge. Built under the code name Y-12 for the atomic bomb project in the early 1940s, the plant was the first at Oak Ridge to go into operation (a division that purified uranium by the more efficient gaseous diffusion process became operational nearly a year later). Y-12 used electromagnetic force to separate the easily fissionable form of uranium, U-235, from nonfissionable U-238. Of the 24,000 people working at the plant, few knew more than the rest of the world what they were making—until August 6, 1945, when the atomic bomb was dropped on Hiroshima, Japan.

to the thriving center of Williamson, one of the transportation centers for "the Billion Dollar Coal Field." Williamson still exists today; but many of these instant communities rose rapidly only to disappear with equal speed. One example was a Kentucky village with the prophetic name of Quicksand. In 1910, a sawmill established there by the Mobray-Robinson Company grew almost overnight into a town, most of whose men were engaged in sawing the great trees of Breathitt County into boards. Mobray-Robinson became the largest producer of hardwood in the world and even opened a branch in Liverpool to accommodate its export trade. But by 1924 the forests were gone, the company was gone, and Quicksand went too. Today there is not even a ghost town.

Was the new city in Tennessee to follow the cycle of "boom-and-bust" or was it significant of a different future? This was only part of the puzzle of those early days at Oak Ridge. From 1943 to 1945, thousands of construction workers were employed in the city—and none of them knew what they were building. What Oak Ridge represented was, of course, a new age of history—the Atomic Age—and the workers there learned of it when the first atom bomb fell on Hiroshima. But for years, at the heart of the Border States, among unsophis-

ticated people who cherished many antique ways, the most sophisticated scientific project of modern times was developed in absolute secrecy.

J. H. Rush, a physicist who worked on the atomic project at Oak Ridge, recalled later, "The people . . . who impressed me most were not the scientists, who knew approximately what they were doing, but the laborers, who didn't. Our experiments often required setting up cumbersome apparatus in situations that involved exposure to atomic radiation. The maintenance men who helped us on such jobs might be required to wear dust masks or to come out of a hazardous area after thirty minutes or an hour, while technicians nosed about with radiation counters. To these laborers —many of them poorly educated men from the local farm country—the intimations of mysterious, invisible danger must have been impressive. Yet I never saw one of them refuse a task, or show any uneasiness in exposing himself to the unknown hazard."

Out of courage and hard work, Oak Ridge burgeoned. Today the Atomic Energy Commission's investment in Tennessee is larger than in any other state—nearly $1.75 billion. The changes these installations can bring to mankind are twofold and contradictory—and typical, too, of the

North Carolina's research triangle

Within the triangle formed by the North Carolina cities of Durham, Chapel Hill and Raleigh *(top)* lies the Border States' leading center for scientific study, Research Triangle Park. Founded in the 1950s, the park provides a tranquil setting for research organizations and easy communication with nearby universities. By 1968 the centers shown below had been built, bringing to the state a cadre of highly trained professionals.

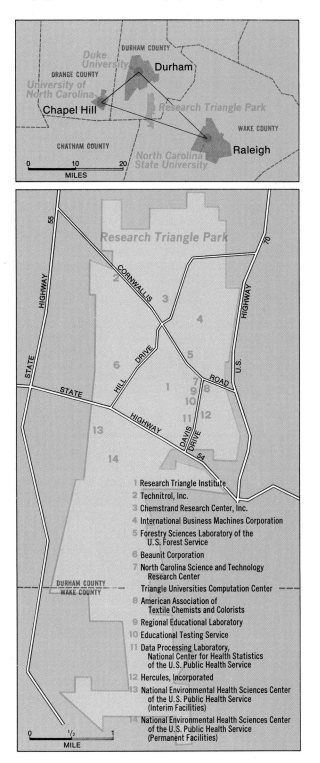

1 Research Triangle Institute
2 Technitrol, Inc.
3 Chemstrand Research Center, Inc.
4 International Business Machines Corporation
5 Forestry Sciences Laboratory of the U.S. Forest Service
6 Beaunit Corporation
7 North Carolina Science and Technology Research Center
  Triangle Universities Computation Center
8 American Association of Textile Chemists and Colorists
9 Regional Educational Laboratory
10 Educational Testing Service
11 Data Processing Laboratory, National Center for Health Statistics of the U.S. Public Health Service
12 Hercules, Incorporated
13 National Environmental Health Sciences Center of the U.S. Public Health Service (Interim Facilities)
14 National Environmental Health Sciences Center of the U.S. Public Health Service (Permanent Facilities)

Border States. For if the most obvious and familiar face of Oak Ridge is destructive, its creative one can unshackle the imagination. Research at the Oak Ridge National Laboratory includes experiments designed to furnish food for starving nations, to rejuvenate aging humans by the use of bone marrow, and to improve the detection and treatment of lung cancer.

When scientist Rush came to evaluate the work at Oak Ridge, he concluded that "the specific horror of atomic war had obscured the real meaning of the Manhattan District Project. What [the project] signified was that mankind was moving into a new order of power over itself and the environment, and that henceforth the consequences of man's acts must be weighed with utmost caution."

Man's self-discipline and the wise use of nature: these challenges are as basic to the Border States as to all the nation. In their patterns of change, however, the Border States still bear their own distinctions. A people and a place that for three long centuries were basically rural and agricultural have become, within three brief decades, largely urban and semi-industrial. Rhythms of life are altering; values are being painfully reassessed.

"How far is it from Oak Ridge to the Great Smokies?" a visitor once asked.

And the answer came back, "About a hundred years."

The answer was accurate. The distances separating places and people of the Border States are often distances of time as much as space. Perhaps more than any other region of the United States, this is the one where yesterday and tomorrow meet. Yesterday has not been completely relinquished, tomorrow has not been fully embraced, and today is taut with the pull between the two. Poised between tradition and change, many of the people seem hopeful of having the best of each.

For the moment, the delicate balance is producing a texture of life in the Border States that is at once vivid and unique—and characterized by contrasts galore. Chapters of the United Daughters of the Confederacy flourish side by side with Newcomers' Clubs in the growing towns. Cow pastures and golf courses, clay-chinked cabins and Dari-Dip drive-ins, used car lots and handicraft shops stud the landscape with contrast. Even the smallest details reflect the larger transformations: grocery stores that carry both *escargots* and black-eyed peas on their shelves, sell canned vichyssoise and hominy grits, feature pickled okra for the cocktail circuit and fresh collard greens for the basic Southern cuisine. And some of the contrasts speak directly of contradictions in the spiritual conditions of the region's people. There are the expensive new brick churches that dot the countryside from Wilmington to Wheeling—and the scattered race-car tracks that culminate in the huge Charlotte Motor Speedway with its World 600 each spring and National 500 each autumn. One observer has spoken of a switch in the region from the "other-worldly" to the "outer-worldly."

These are only a few of the manifestations of change in the Border States—and change creates problems. It is easier to determine when to replace an obsolete mule than an obsolete attitude, and that very fact gives rise to some of the social and political anachronisms of the region. People who live in a city and use all its gadgets but retain rural habits and values are bound to have trouble in the modern world.

One area of trouble is the peculiarly modern field of labor relations. In the Border States' coal mines and textile mills, labor unions have been persistent and aggressive in their attempts to organize the unorganized. Yet an astute North Carolina journalist, Roy Parker Jr., analyzed his state's attitudes toward unions in this way: "The mental makeup of the typical Tar Heel working man makes him fundamentally hard to organize. And once organized, difficult for his union to serve. Arbitrators say that the bulk of day-to-day problems which they are called on by management to settle grow out of this mental makeup which is a product of the workers' background."

Some of the consequences of the workers' mental makeup stem from generations of rural freedom and rural demands. When the fish are jumping, a worker will go fishing; at hog-killing or tobacco-harvesting time, he will leave his factory job for as long as he is needed at home. And on the job, he will ignore or defy any order or request that seems unjust to him. Such workers, as Parker says, are "freedom-loving critters, as jealous of their right to fish—or tell off a foreman—as they are desirous of their weekly paycheck."

In a deeper sense, the pattern of a worker's life may lead him to resist unionization and the habits of an industrial age. Typically, the head of a family cultivates his own small holding of tobacco or cotton land in the evening and weekend hours left to him by his job. Similarly, a woman who goes to work often commutes from her family farm. "For such people," Parker concludes, "the rough-and-tumble of union organization and ac-

tivity has little charm, and few feel the benefits which unionization could bring are really worth the trouble. Where a union exists, they sometimes dissipate on personal and petty grievances the power and good-will that will be needed later to carry really important questions."

In another highly controversial area, that of race relations, the character of the Border States people has played an obstructive part in white adjustment to desegregation. A social scientist who moved from Massachusetts to central North Carolina summed up one aspect of this problem in an open letter to his new Tar Heel neighbors: "I have decided that it is, ironically, one of the South's most endearing virtues—a warm and wonderful sense of hospitality—that finally stands in the way of visualizing hopefully a social arrangement in which Negroes exercise their full civic rights. Southerners are so warm-heartedly accustomed to thinking that any friend must be invited to dinner that when they imagine equality of opportunity between the races they immediately think they must open their homes to Negroes. . . . Somehow we former Yankees ought to be able to pass the word that the granting to all citizens of their civil rights does not . . . mean that we must invite them to share our bed and board." Yet the very warmth and totality of commitment that characterize the Border States people lead some residents to believe that when a majority of their neighbors do accept the reality as well as the rhetoric of racial equality, race relations may become more harmonious here than in any other region of the country.

Reflected in both labor and racial relations is one of the basic contradictions within the Border States today: the clash between an impersonal, analytical society and a highly personal, intuitive people. At times the character of the people, for all its color and warmth, impairs the functioning of the society. The president of a small college in West Virginia, himself a native of the Border States, has spoken with real anguish of this problem: "An outsider would have difficulty believing how completely every issue in this college, this town, this county and this state becomes a personal issue. Voting is on personalities rather than philosophies. County government is incredibly personalized, even to the school system which is often the biggest industry in the county. At the community level there is little sustained effort. Ad hoc committees may form to meet momentary problems, but as soon as that purpose is accomplished, they disband. Again, everything becomes

Children at play on a sandy putting green at Pinehurst, North Carolina, around 1910 suggest the resort's early attraction for golfers of all ages—and symbolize the Border States' long-recognized potential as a recreation area. Established as a health resort in 1895 by Boston industrialist James Walker Tufts,

Pinehurst got its first golf course four years later, with putting greens of hard-packed sand. By 1961 Tufts' successors had rounded out a total of five courses—all with grass greens—and Pinehurst had become the host for amateur golf tournaments. Today the resort retains its atmosphere of elegant serenity.

personal. And this reinforces the reluctance to assume leadership, because then an individual is in a position to be blamed for any misunderstanding, and this may carry over to his family and all aspects of his daily life."

This educator has touched upon the most profound need of the Border States today: the need for leadership. Aubrey Wagner, chairman of the board of TVA, said not long ago that one of his organization's greatest shortcomings has been its failure to find and involve leaders "and put our tools in their hands." This has been, in varying degrees, the failure of every other institution in the Border States, and the need of leadership is a recurring theme in every discussion of the region.

At this point the region's dilemmas and those of the nation converge. The big problems of the Border States are also American problems; they are shaped by the region's history and characteristics, but they are essentially American. In the Border States, two of the most pressing of these problems can be presented as questions:

First, can Americans govern themselves—or more specifically, can they achieve a viable politics at the local level, insuring strong roots for their federal system?

Second, can Americans conserve their natural environment sufficiently to preserve their own lives?

As though in answer to that first question, there have been significant changes at the state level throughout the Border States. Only a few years ago, two of the Border States were politically controlled by two of the strongest machines in the United States. In Tennessee the highly personal Democratic organization headed by Edward H. Crump directly controlled the city of Memphis and the rest of Shelby County; through his control of a decisive bloc of votes, his domination of the state party machinery and his ability to make deals with east Tennessee Republicans, Crump also ran the entire state. Candidates for governor, senator, and congressman generally "talked with Memphis" and "Mister Crump" before launching their campaigns. But two men, Senators Estes Kefauver and Albert Gore, were not under the control of the machine, and their rise in politics marked Crump's decline. At his death in 1954 he left no successor, and the organization's strength on the state level was dissipated.

In Virginia the power of Senator Harry F. Byrd was so deeply woven into the social, economic and political fabric of the state that the Old Dominion was sometimes called "Byrdland." The percentage of the electorate who voted at the polls was among the lowest for any state in the nation. When Francis Pickens Miller ran for governor in opposition to the Byrd candidate, a white laborer whose vote he solicited replied, "Why Colonel, you know I don't belong to the folks who vote." In 1966, however, two Byrd Congressional patriarchs who had accumulated impressive seniority in both the Senate and the House of Representatives were defeated by younger men, both campaigning on the argument that "It's time for Virginia to move into the 20th Century."

Tom Wicker of *The New York Times,* himself a native of North Carolina, discussed the defeat of one of the Byrd candidates, Congressman Howard Smith, in terms of a changing world and, more particularly, a changing electorate. Noting that in 36 years of Congressional service Smith had seen "the rise of Big Government, Big Labor, Big Defense, Big Welfare and even Bigger Business than the world knew in his youth," Wicker listed some of the forces for change that had passed the Congressman by: "Technology, communications, urbanization, a depression, a World War, a cold war." He ended his analysis by describing the newest and strongest force in modern Virginia politics: "Perhaps none of these things has changed Judge Smith's particular world more than the emergence to a new vitality of the Negroes of the South. Few developments more rapidly eroded the immense power he once wielded as the leader of Southern Democrats in the House."

At the state and local levels, the task of achieving broadly based and responsive government is far from completed. Historian Dewey Grantham has succinctly described the basic nature of the task, not only in the Border States, but in many other parts of the nation: "The problem everywhere is how to quicken the interest of the voters in state politics, how to recruit able people to go into state and local government, and how to make the political process at these levels more responsive to the actual differences and divisions of the people and to the majority opinion."

One leader of the Border States who has addressed himself to this problem is a former governor of North Carolina, Terry Sanford. Under his administration, an innovative state government gave North Carolina a new thrust in its public education; founded the North Carolina School of the Arts, which discovers and develops artistic talent in the youth of the region; and created the North Carolina Fund, the first state-level, non-profit organization set up primarily to experiment

with, and demonstrate new approaches to, the problem of poverty.

The scope of these programs can be indicated by a partial list of specific achievements. In higher education, North Carolina created three new senior colleges and set up the machinery for a system of two-year community colleges. In the public schools, teachers' salaries were raised and additional teachers were hired for unusual students: the academically talented, the mentally retarded, the hard-of-hearing, the visually handicapped and the physically disabled. A vocational school teaches trades to youthful first-offenders in prison, and educational researchers are strengthening requirements for prospective teachers, expanding the role of educational television and revising the school curriculum.

The North Carolina Fund, the state's major antipoverty agency, carries on an even wider range of activities. Incorporated in 1963, the Fund is financed by an intricate combination of foundation grants, matching local contributions and state appropriations. It cooperates with the educational establishment to improve instruction in the first three grades (educators agree that a prime cause of school dropouts is inadequate training in those grades) and in combating adult illiteracy. In the rural counties, workers for the Fund help train federal volunteers and work along with them on sanitation and housing projects, nursing programs and community improvements. Throughout the state, these workers act as a force for progressive change, involving the poor in the problems of their own rehabilitation, confronting racial issues at their most intense, trying to find bridges across the chasm between incredible poverty and the incalculable wealth of regional resources.

At lower levels of government, progress has been slower. One of the thorniest political problems in the Border States has been the failure of city and county governments, in both urban and rural areas, to work together. As one Tennessee journalist said, "The biggest challenge our region has to face up to is this one of cooperation. Epidemics, urban sprawl, air pollution—all spill over the lines and affect everyone. Yet it's still hard to get the towns and counties to work together on the most basic needs."

Thus the tensions arising from rapid change continue to affect all aspects of life in the Border States. Happily, many changes in state government have been good ones. In cultural matters, the region has provided a model for the nation. North

Carolina was the first of the states to provide substantial public funds to build an art collection for its people. Kentucky was a leader among the states in the use of the "bookmobile"; as early as the first decade of this century, pack mules laden with books brought literature to the isolated back country of the state. Virginia's unique Barter Theater was the first state-supported theater in the nation and Virginia was the first state to initiate an "artmobile."

And what of the natural environment—the second great problem of the Border States? Natural resources acknowledge no man-made boundaries. Water yields to no state borders, air knows no county lines, mountains and woods are confined to no individual community or set of communities. One of the biggest changes of the past decade has been the increased awareness within the Border States of the need to conserve, and in some instances restore, natural resources. Yet, as in education, health, industry and many other areas, the region must run merely to stand still. Destruction of its richest, most fragile resources has been going on for generations; at best, it is difficult to reverse the tide.

A report issued by the West Virginia Conservation Commission could apply to all the region. The state, it said, "has not, up to the present time, done much with its scenery except to mar it, mutilate it, and burn it up. Except in the case of mineral springs, practically nothing has been done in this State to make scenery attractive or to bring it to the attention of the outside world. . . . A good many things must be done before West Virginia will take its due rank as a resort for tourists, healthseekers, and sightseers. It must first protect its woods and make them attractive. It must clean its streams and stock them with fish, and make and enforce civilized laws for protection of the fish. It must stop the senseless slaughter of birds and game. It must build roads that can be traveled with speed and safety by modern vehicles. In building these roads the value of scenery must be considered in regions where scenery is attractive."

That was not written this year or last year, but six decades ago, in 1908. Significantly, that conservation commission was disbanded after it had issued this one report, and West Virginia refused to join the conservation movement led by Theodore Roosevelt. Though the nation's first school of forestry was founded in the Border States in 1898, the region as a whole has allowed its trees to be demolished, its waters to be poisoned and its air to be polluted with only the faintest of protests.

Slowly, however, the picture is changing. Now, when more than 6 million visits are made annually to the green heights of the Great Smokies National Park, and when the Blue Ridge Parkway of Virginia and North Carolina has become the most popular national park facility in the country, the region has begun to realize that its natural beauty is a permanent treasure, not merely a temporary asset for exploitation. Rivers and streams loaded with municipal and industrial wastes are being partially reclaimed and their dead waters restored to a degree of life. Most recently of all, the air itself is being studied, its foulness measured and its purity appraised. But in each of these areas of conservation, progress moves by inches to counteract destruction that often swept through natural resources like an avalanche, and the decision to preserve an environment in which man can live fully depends upon the conscience and commitment of all the region's and the country's people.

A Border States writer, Thomas Wolfe, recognized the deep divisions and daily betrayals of his region, yet voiced its hope and vigor. Just before his death in 1938, Wolfe wrote: "I think the true discovery of America is before us. I think the true fulfillment of our spirit, of our people, of our mighty and immortal land, is yet to come. I think the true discovery of our own democracy is still before us. And I think that all these things are certain as the morning, as inevitable as noon. I think I speak for most men living when I say that our America is Here, is Now, . . . and that this glorious assurance is not only our living hope, but our dream to be accomplished."

Accomplishing a dream is no mean task. But the people of the Border States have been dreaming and struggling for more than three centuries. As a place to pursue an ideal, the region may well be what one of its first settlers, Ralph Lane, called it back in 1585—"the goodliest soile under the cope of heaven." Personal relationships between man and man, between man and nature, are still possible here. Men have been forging the philosophy and perfecting the functioning of democracy here for a long time, too. They have had noble successes and tragic failures, but it is not likely that they will allow their vigorous past to become a millstone rather than a steppingstone. From the first settlement at Jamestown to the new city at Oak Ridge, the real border character of the region has always been between yesterday and tomorrow. Today it is also one of mankind's frontiers.

Three yearlings, untried at the race track but already worth thousands of dollars, canter across a pasture at Leslie Combs's Spendthrift Farm.

A horse farm
in the Bluegrass

The beautiful, rolling country around Lexington, Kentucky, might have been created for the purpose of breeding and raising race horses. Its soil nourishes forage with the minerals necessary for a horse's growth and strength, and its gently flowing streams provide fresh, clean water. On farm after farm, miles of board fence divide lush pastures of Kentucky bluegrass. These pastures have produced most of the immortals of American racing, including Man o' War, Citation and Native Dancer.

One of the most successful Kentuckians raising Thoroughbred horses—the breed that dominates racing throughout the world—is Leslie Combs II, owner of Spendthrift Farm. Combs races few of his own horses; he keeps most of them until they are only a year old and sells the best of these yearlings. For two decades horses bred at Spendthrift Farm have brought high prices from buyers who gamble that a Spendthrift yearling will win back its cost and then some.

Photographs by Richard Meek

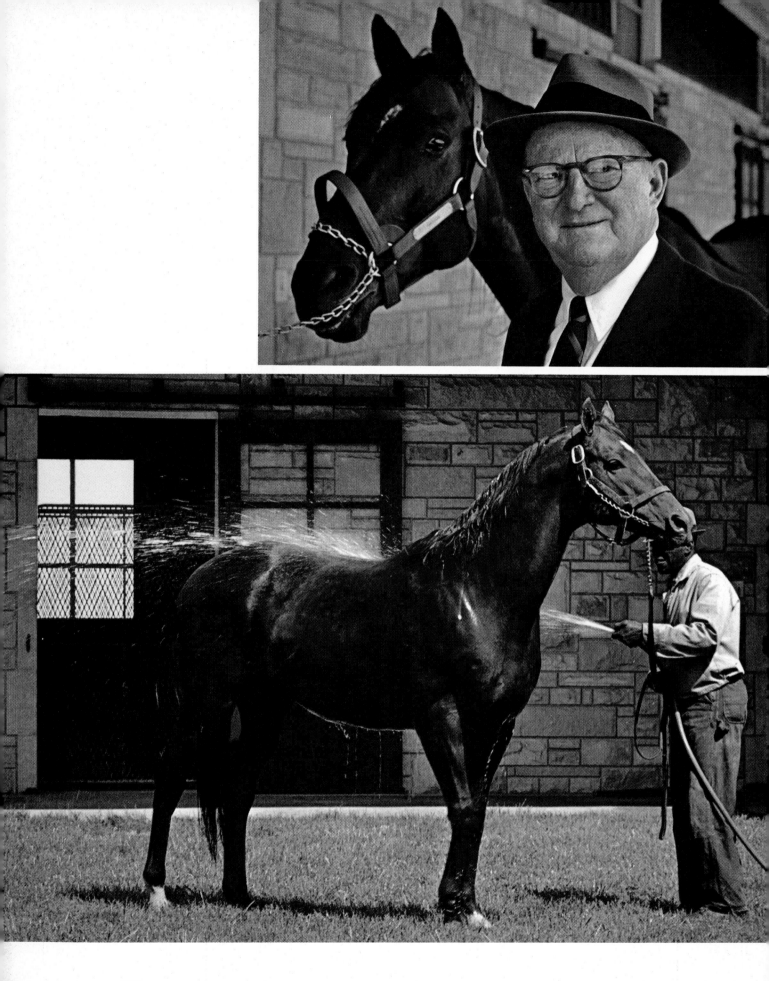

A big business in a pastoral setting

Spendthrift Farm got its name from a horse—a colt that Combs's great grandfather mockingly named "Spendthrift," after his wife. (She got even by naming another horse "Miser," after her husband.) But the name is misleading, for this farm is no mere hobby. Combs, who is at once an inspired breeder of horses and a shrewd businessman, started in 1937 with 127 acres and eight mares. Today his farm *(below),* with its complex of central buildings and outlying fields, covers some 5,000 acres and houses 250 horses. About 75 of the horses belong to Combs and his associates; the rest are boarders, mostly mares that have been sent to Spendthrift to be bred to the illustrious stallions in permanent residence there.

The most valuable horses on the farm are these stallions, about 40 in number. Two of the greatest stallions in the world live at

Spendthrift: Nashua, shown with Mr. Combs in the picture at the left, and Swaps, seen at bottom left being hosed down at the end of the day. Between them Nashua and Swaps ran off with the racing world's famous "Triple Crown" in 1955, when Nashua won the Preakness and Belmont Stakes, and Swaps the Kentucky Derby. Nashua alone cost $1,251,200.

His stallions and other people's mares are not Combs's only concern: he gives equal attention to the raising and breeding of his own mares. Combs has had uncanny success in mating the right mare to the right stallion at the right time: he has repeatedly bred a foal of higher quality than either of its parents. But he does not rely on instinct alone. Inspiration is backed up by modern scientific methods and a businesslike attention to every detail *(following pages).*

The varied day of an assistant farm manager

7:30 A.M. Early on a spring morning, Tommy Curd, one of Spendthrift Farm's two assistant managers, uses a two-way radio to check out his day's assignments with the farm manager. All of the farm's 25 trucks are equipped with such radios. One of 175 Spendthrift employees (some others wait at the truck window for his orders), Curd has charge of a section of the farm and of training yearlings.

8:30 A.M. As a stallion is led into a shed full of mares, Curd prepares to make notes on mares that are responsive and ready to be bred. Such mares will be taken to a breeding barn to be mated with prize Spendthrift studs. About 250 mares will bear foals during the spring, and each mare will be bred within a few days after foaling.

7:30 A.M.

8:30 A.M.

11:00 A.M.

1:30 P.M.

9:30 A.M. Carrying his notebook out to a pasture, Curd checks the physical condition of some of the horses in his charge. Every horse is inspected at least once a day for signs of injury and disease. Serious problems are referred to the veterinarian, on call 24 hours a day. Minor problems such as nutrition, causing a horse to be thin or weak, are diagnosed on the spot and treated with individually mixed feeds.

11:00 A.M. Curd and Combs watch as a boarding mare is inspected by its owners. When this picture was made, the mare was close to foaling; a few days later a fine bay colt was born. Many mares boarding at Spendthrift Farm are owned by well-known individuals and racing stables; clients have included Louis B. Mayer and Elizabeth Arden.

1:30 P.M. Curd watches one of the horses in his charge getting a workout on the farm's half-mile training track. Although Spendthrift Farm races few of its horses, a number of two-year-old fillies are sent to the track each year in the hope that they will win important races and thus enhance their value and that of their foals.

2:30 P.M. Curd and Dr. A. H. Davidson make an X-ray picture of the leg of a two-year-old injured in training. Thoroughbreds are exceptionally frail horses, for all their speed and power, and they often crack or chip ankle and leg bones while galloping on a training track. Such minor injuries usually heal in time, but a horse that suffers them in its youth may never run as fast afterward.

9:30 A.M.

2:30 P.M.

The nation's finest yearlings

The high point of the year at Spendthrift Farm comes in early summer, when its best one-year-olds are sold at auction. The profit or loss from a whole year's work rests upon the prices brought by these horses at a sale, and every precaution is taken in readying the horses for their moment of commercial truth. Fragile and skittish, the horses require constant attention to prevent them from injuring themselves or one another.

From the time Spendthrift foals are born, Leslie Combs begins to select about 30 perfect animals for the most prestigious auction of them all—the Keeneland sale, at Lexington. Keeneland's managers accept only animals with flawless pedigrees and superb builds, and competition is intense. To help him decide upon the horses he will send there, Combs

receives monthly written reports from his farm manager and veterinarian on every foal and yearling at Spendthrift. He also gets advice from the nation's most eminent Thoroughbred appraiser, Humphrey Finney *(wearing a cap),* who is shown inspecting a colt in the picture at bottom right. Each male yearling selected for Keeneland is turned out into a separate paddock *(below);* on especially bright days it is kept in a barn so that the sun will not bleach its coat. Happily, all this painstaking care is rewarded: Spendthrift Farm yearlings bring the highest prices at nearly every sale.

Even the yearlings who do not go to the Keeneland sale, like the two shown running free in the picture at right, are fine horses. Sold at relatively obscure sales, they often go on to great success on the track.

In the cool of a spring morning a tiny foal, only two weeks old, frolics in a pasture. The love of running is so strong in Thoroughbreds that they

egin to race after their mothers when only a few hours old, almost as if to strengthen their legs for more strenuous racing in their maturity.